CURL
TO WIN

CURL
TO WIN

Expert Advice to Improve Your Game

RUSS HOWARD

With a foreword by Brad Gushue

Collins

Published by HarperCollins Publishers Ltd.

First Edition

HarperCollins books may be purchased for educational, business, or sales promotional use through our Special Markets Department.

HarperCollins Publishers Ltd
2 Bloor Street East, 20th Floor
Toronto, Ontario, Canada
M4W 1A8

www.harpercollins.ca

Library and Archives Canada Cataloguing in Publication

Howard, Russ
Curl to win : expert advice to improve your game / Russ Howard; foreword by Brad Gushue. – 1st ed.

ISBN 978-0-00-200848-8

1. Curling. I. Title.

GV845.H69 2009   796.964   C2007-903541-8

Printed in the United States
PHO 9 8 7 6 5 4 3 2 1

To Team Howard
Barb, Bill, Glenn, Wendy, Steven, and Ashley

CONTENTS

FOREWORD

BY

BRAD GUSHUE

2006 OLYMPIC GOLD MEDALLIST, MEN'S CURLING

THE FIRST CURLING GAME I ever watched on television was the final of the 1987 Labatt Brier between Russ Howard and Bernie Sparkes. I don't remember much about the game, but I do remember becoming hooked on curling. Ever since that game, I have been a fan of Russ Howard. His skill, intensity, and knowledge of curling are unmatched. The way he curls and the innovations he has brought to the sport of curling have improved the game for curlers of every generation.

I enjoyed much success early in my career, and through a combination of hard work and a burning desire to win I was able to envision competing in the 2006 Olympics. When Russ Howard agreed to join our squad in May 2005, I knew for sure we were capable of winning gold. With Russ on our team, we had a tremendous opportunity to tap into one of the top minds in curling.

From the moment Russ came on board, it became obvious to me why he is so widely regarded as one of the best curlers ever to play the game. His attention to detail, his determination, and his unwavering quest to get better each and every game were contagious. We used to have a lot of fun at Russ's expense about his age, but we were always amazed that he never slowed down. He was always tinkering with his delivery to make it more consistent and reliable under pressure. It didn't stop when we got to Turin, either. Even at the Olympics, he was trying to find ways to improve his shot making and get more curl with his delivery.

Of course, you need not aspire to a national or Olympic championship in order to benefit from Russ's book. Whether you are a weekend warrior, local league member, or indeed a provincial-, national-, or international-level athlete, you will become a better curler—a winning curler—after reading *Curl to Win*.

ix

INTRODUCTION

I REMEMBER SPENDING MANY a Saturday night as a boy in Midland, Ontario, sitting by the television and watching my beloved Toronto Maple Leafs. Even in those early days, I knew that I would somehow make my mark on the ice; what I didn't know was that it would ultimately be in the sport of curling.

From the very first time I stepped in the hack, I felt my best. No matter what else was happening in my life, the moment I stepped on a sheet of ice I felt at home. I loved the competition, the camaraderie, and the way the game challenged me to get better each and every time out.

I have had the privilege to experience the game from various positions: adviser, advocate, athlete, and nervous father. All have led me to a greater appreciation of the amazing sport of curling.

When I was younger, my dad spent hours with my brother Glenn and me, teaching us the basics and helping us take our game to the next level. Now my children, Ashley and Steven, have taken up curling at a competitive level too.

Curling is an intricate game that, when played well, is beautiful in its simplicity. In *Curl to Win,* we will look at how you can improve in everything from throwing and sweeping to shot selection, strategy, and finding your place on a team. Of course, my book would not be complete without a look at the four-rock free guard zone rule that Glenn and I pioneered in 1989. The free guard zone is where games are won and lost, and I will take you through it step by step.

In curling, as in any other sport, consistency should be your goal, but always allow yourself to have fun while you improve. Trust me, if you are having fun, you'll play better.

GETTING STARTED

GENERAL INFO FOR THE NOVICE CURLER

"Not once, in everything I've done,
have I ever felt the same wonder and humanity
as when I'm playing the game of curling."
—from the movie *Men with Brooms*

CURLING ISN'T HARD TO DO; it's just hard to do well and consistently. The same can be said about the equally addictive pastime of hitting a golf ball. Curling, however, has a number of advantages over golf: your equipment costs are minimal, and membership fees or pay-as-you-play costs are low. Like golf, it can be a sport for life, from "Little Rock" for kids to "stick curling" for those in their golden years who need a delivery device to play.

Curlers of every age can go to their nearest curling club and find not only a warm welcome from a very friendly group but also a social hub. You can curl at any level, from recreational curling through club curling to competitive curling.

It is no surprise that many curlers, as I am, are also passionate golfers. There are fundamental similarities between the two great Scottish games. Each requires that players be honourable and honest, that they police themselves. And each game begins and ends with a handshake. Both golf and curling require that you adapt to changing conditions, be prepared for adversity, maximize your advantages, and employ a well-thought-out strategy while capitalizing on opportunities.

EQUIPMENT

One of the wonderful things about the sport of curling is that you don't have to spend a great deal of money to get started.

Let's start from the ground up and take a look at footwear. For the novice, a simple running shoe with a clean surface and good removable gripper will do just fine. You can slip a slider over one shoe (your slider foot)—these can often be provided by the curling club. Or you can purchase curling shoes with the slider built right in.

For those

When choosing curling shoes, remember that the thickness of the Teflon affects your balance and sliding distance. For maximum speed, thicker Teflon is recommended. If you're starting out, a thinner slider will still give you some speed, but will help your balance. The circular recess in the sole of the shoe can improve your balance and stability.

of you playing at the competitive level, the type of footwear you use is very important. Be conscious of the thickness of the Teflon slider that you are using, because the thicker the slider, the farther you will go. You'll slide more slowly with a slider $\frac{1}{16}$ inch thick than the quarter-inch-thick slider I use, but a thinner, slower slider will help your balance and safety.

In terms of clothing, flexibility is key. It is very hard to be able to get the kind of flexibility you need if you're wearing jeans. I suggest that you look at buying a proper pair of pants specifically designed for curling. In addition to flexibility, warmth and comfort are essential. Ideally, you'll want to wear layers and a warm jacket in a colder setting—that way, if you're overdressed you can always remove a layer.

As far as gloves are concerned, you can purchase curling gloves that resemble baseball batting gloves. The glove will provide the kind of grip that you want, which is as much about feel as anything else. You may have to try out a few types before you find the one you like. I suggest a vinyl glove for novices, while those who play more often

If your curling club is on the cold side, insulated gloves or mitts are the ticket.

will favour a more expensive leather glove.

Finally, let's take a look at brooms and brushes. The straw and push brooms that were standard years ago have largely been replaced by interchangeable swivel-head brushes. Because sweepers can now adjust their brushes, they can sweep at the most effective angle and change their brush heads to suit ice conditions.

The cost of brushes can vary widely, especially when it comes to the handle. The biggest difference between the wooden- or plastic-handle and the graphite-handle push broom is weight. This may not seem like a big deal if you're playing only once or twice a week, but when you are involved in a

THE BRUSH

If you're not maintaining your brush, you could be wasting your time sweeping.

A nylon brush head is very effective when it's brand new, but with every end you play, it becomes less effective. If you're playing recreationally at your club, you may change your brush head once a month. At a major championship, our team will use new heads every game. Depending on the ice conditions, you may even change your heads two or three times a game. Arena ice, for example, tends to become frosty, so the nylon head will get damp and be less effective. A dirty or damp brush will not create the desired friction.

week-long tournament where you are expected to play 10 to 15 games, the advantage of a lighter broom is invaluable.

Once you've got your broom and shoes, you're ready to step out onto the ice.

THE SHEET

The ice shed in a curling club is divided into sheets of ice separated by sidelines or physical barriers. A rock that touches the sidelines or barriers must be removed from play. At either end of the sheet is a target-like set of concentric rings known as "the house." The house is made up of four concentric circles with diameters of one, four, eight, and twelve feet. The one-foot circle in the centre of the house is called "the button," while the other three circles are commonly referred to by their diameters: the four-foot, the eight-foot, and the twelve foot. The goal in curling is essentially to get as many of your rocks closer to the button than your opponent does.

Sheets can vary from club to club. A curling sheet is 146 feet long and up to 15 feet, 7 inches wide in international play (the norm in Canada is 14 feet, 2 inches), with a line down the centre (centre line), a line across the back of the house (back line), and a perpendicular line that runs through the centre of the house (tee line). A double footrest (the hack) is placed on the centre line, 12 feet behind the centre of each house. Two lines, each of them four inches wide, are painted across the sheet 21 feet in front of the centre of the house. These are called "hog lines." When a rock is thrown, it must be clearly released before it crosses the near hog line, and it must completely cross the hog line at the far end to remain in play.

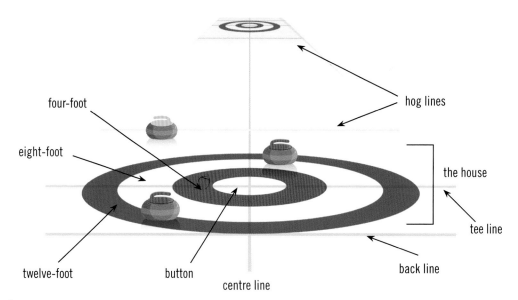

four-foot

eight-foot

hog lines

the house

tee line

twelve-foot

button

back line

centre line

THE ICE

Curling ice is different from hockey ice—there are no Zambonis in curling. The surface of a hockey rink, at least at the beginning of the game, is smooth. Icemakers in curling clubs, on the other hand, cover the ice with a fine spray of water that freezes into little droplets. This is called "the pebble."

The pebble minimizes the rock's contact with the flat ice, thereby allowing the rock to slide much farther and straighter. As the game progresses and the sharp tops of the pebble start to wear down, the reverse happens: rocks encounter more friction, slow down, and curl more.

In a perfect world, every ice surface used for curling would be the same. In Canada, we are lucky to have the best icemaking facilities and ice technicians in the world, but ice surfaces still differ from club to club and sheet to sheet and—most important—minute to minute. If you want to become a better curler, become a master of the art of reading the ice and making it work for you. This is perhaps the most important factor in the game.

THE ROCKS

Curling rocks weigh nearly 40 pounds, including the handle, and are made of

The entire curling rock is highly polished except for the striking band and running surface. When two rocks collide, the rough striking band's gear effect causes the rocks to spin in opposite directions.

striking band

granite. They may be no more than 36 inches in circumference, and no taller than 4½ inches. Parts of the rock—the bottom and the striking band around the middle—are not polished. Under the rock's pressure, the ice surface melts ever so slightly and forms a very thin layer of water on top of the ice; this supports the rock and enables it to travel a very long distance relative to the force applied to it. Consider how far you could throw a 40-pound lump of granite in a hockey rink: it wouldn't be anywhere near the length of a curling sheet from hack to button. All rocks are designed to revolve, and will tend to curve in the direction in which they are revolving, but different rocks

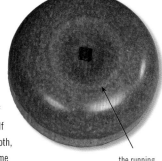

The bottom of a curling rock. The centre, the running cup, is concave. The rough running surface surrounding the running cup is the only part of the rock that touches the ice. If the running surface were smooth, rocks wouldn't curl, so the game would be called "straighting."

the running surface

will curl to a different degree—some more, some less. The more you play, the easier it will become to identify the individual characteristics of a rock.

TEAM

You will quickly find out that no matter what the skill level of a player is, it takes a team of four, playing in harmony, to succeed. Curling is unique in that 25 per cent of the team has to contribute 100 per cent of the time.

A team consists of four players. In a major championship, there may be five, with one designated as a substitute. Your lineup can change from game to game, as can the players' positions. But the rotation cannot be changed during a game, unless there is an injury. Each player delivers two rocks, with opposing teams alternating, for a total of eight rocks per team.

The names of the positions on the team refer to the order in which the rocks are thrown: first rock, or lead; second rock, or second; third rock, also the mate or vice-skip; and fourth rock, or skip. All positions are equally important—it is just as vital for the lead to set up the opening and the second to develop the game as it is for the mate to consolidate scoring opportunities and the skip to put in the scoring or bailout shots.

The skip is the team captain and strategist, with the final word on the direction of the game for the team. The skip may play in any position in the delivery rotation. When it is the skip's turn to deliver, he must designate a teammate to act as skip.

The two teams toss a coin before the game, and the winner chooses whether to throw first or last. The team that throws the first rock has the choice of colour. The winner of the coin toss would, normally, choose to have the advantage of last rock (the "hammer"). But many times, I have given up last-rock advantage to choose rock colour, knowing that one set of rocks is more consistent than the other.

THE GAME

The objective of the game is to score more points than your opponent over the course of eight ends of play (some major competitions are still 10 ends). Each team throws eight rocks in each end, and only the team closest to the centre of the house can score. Multiple points are scored if two or more rocks of the same colour are closer than any of the opposing team's rocks.

KEEPING SCORE

Scoring in curling is pretty simple—it is the scoreboard that causes all the confusion!

KEEPING SCORE

THE TRADITIONAL CURLING SCOREBOARD can be confusing, but once you get the hang of reading it, you'll find that one glance is all it takes to figure out the score of the game, how many ends have been completed, and which team has the last rock in the next end (the "hammer").

In this example, at the end of the first end, Team Yellow has scored one point because its rock is closer to the button than any of the three blue rocks in the rings.

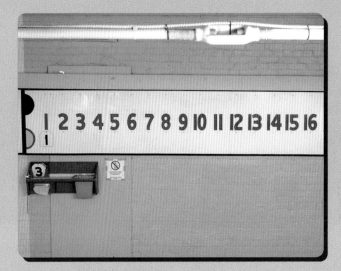

On the scoreboard, the centre row, or score line, represents the number of points. Because Yellow scored one point in the first end, the end number 1 is hung in its row beneath the red score number 1. This tells us that Yellow leads, 1–0, after the first end. Yellow will throw first in the second end, giving Blue the last-rock advantage.

In the second end, each team had three rocks in the rings, but all of Yellow's are closer to the button than any of Blue's, so they all count. Yellow scores three points.

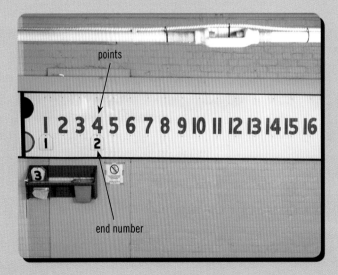

points

1 2 3 4 5 6 7 8 9 10 11 12 13 14 15 16

end number

On the scoreboard, the end number 2 is hung beneath the red 4. Yellow has a 4–0 lead, and Blue has the hammer in the third end.

Another crowded house! In the third end, Blue has come back strongly, with four rocks in scoring position.

Accordingly, the end number 3 is placed in Blue's row, above the red 4. At the end of three ends, the score is tied 4–4, and Yellow has last rock in the fourth end.

MEASURING

In curling, you often may not be able to see which team's rocks are closer to the button. There are two types of measuring devices used in curling: the biter measure and the dial measure. Each has its own purpose.

BITER MEASURE OR "SIX-FOOT MEASURE"

The biter measure is fairly simple: it's a six-foot-long bar used to determine whether a rock is touching ("biting") the 12-foot ring. The pointed end is placed in the tee—the centre of the house—and if the end of the bar touches the rock, we know the rock is in the house. The biter measure can be used at the completion of an end for scoring. It can also be used during an end to determine if a rock is in play when the rock is at the very back of the house on the centre line.

DIAL MEASURE

Here, we have a dial measure. It's used to determine which of two rocks is closest to the button, and may be used only at the completion of an end.

The measure is then rotated clockwise towards the first rock, and a measurement is taken. Curling rocks aren't all the same diameter, so we always measure the edge nearest the button. In this case, we get a reading of 2.0.

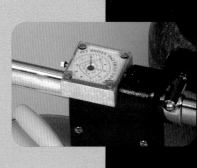

The process is repeated for the second rock. Here, a reading of 1.5 is recorded, so Blue is closer than Yellow.

In order to be "in play," a rock must completely cross the hog line, not touch either sideline or divider, and not completely cross the back line.

Only one team can score points per end —the team with the rocks closest to the button.

In order to be "in play," a rock must completely cross the hog line, not touch either sideline or divider, and not completely cross the back line. If the rock is not in play, it is removed from the sheet. Any rock that is "biting" (touching outer ring) or is actually in the house is eligible to be counted for points, but only those rocks that are closer to the button than the nearest opposition rock count. At the completion of the end, if you can't see which team's rock is closest to the button, you can then measure the two rocks to determine the closest. If for example, yellow is counting and you are measuring for a possible second point and the measure is tied, then yellow will score only one.

GENERAL RULES AND ETIQUETTE

Curling is played according to one of two basic sets of rules. One set is for non-officiated general play (club play, in essence) and the other for officiated, or competitive, play. For the complete Canadian Curling Association rules, please see the appendix. Here are the basics to get you started.

A game starts and ends with a handshake.

Delivery
- Be ready when it's your turn to throw.
- Be courteous, allowing space for your opponent to throw.
- Clearly release your rock before the near hog line.
- If, for whatever reason, you want to stop your delivery motion, you can re-throw the rock as long as it has not reached the near tee line.
- After you've thrown your rock, it's common to put your hands on the ice for stability; this can melt the ice pebble. Be courteous towards the icemaker, and avoid touching the ice with any part of your body for any length of time.

Sweeping

- Sweepers should stay between hog lines when the other team is throwing.
- If you happen to touch a running rock before the far hog line, it is considered "burned" and is taken out of play.
- Between tee lines, all members of the delivering team can sweep their own rock. Behind the tee line, only one player from each team can sweep.
- Give the thrower space and don't crowd him.
- Your job is to control the speed of the rock. It's the skip's job to call the direction.
- Don't clean your brush over the ice surface.
- It's illegal to damage the ice surface with any part of your equipment.

Free Guard Zone

- The free guard zone is the area between the hog line and the tee line, not including the house.
- You can move, but not remove from play, your opponent's first two rocks if they're in the free guard zone. It's not until the fifth rock of the end that you can remove your opponent's rocks, but you can remove your own rocks in the free guard zone.

- If one of your first four rocks thrown removes your opponent's rock from the free guard zone, the delivered rock is taken out of play, and all affected rocks are returned to their original positions.

THE FIVE KEYS TO BEING A WINNING CURLER

WHETHER YOU'RE JUST STARTING OUT or have been curling for as long as I have, there five key factors to improving your game.

1. SLIDE STRAIGHT TO YOUR TARGET

You need a balanced delivery to slide straight and hit the target (the broom). Even a little drift off line during your delivery can cause you to miss your target by a huge margin, by the time your rock reaches the far end.

Sandra Schmirler's flawless delivery made her one the best female curlers who ever played the sport.

2. DON'T UNDERESTIMATE SWEEPING

Every successful team has great sweepers. The thrower has control of the rock for only the first four seconds. Sweepers have control for the last 24 seconds. On perfect ice conditions, two good sweepers can help a rock travel as much as five to six feet farther; sweeping can also keep takeout shots a little straighter.

3. KNOW HOW TO READ THE ICE

Ice conditions can affect how far a rock travels and how much it curls. Even the perfect delivery won't do any good if you haven't paid close attention to ice conditions throughout the game. The best teams in the world have four players that read the ice well.

4. CONTROL THE FRONT

Most battles are won or lost in front of the rings, not in them. Remember, if your rock stops in front of the rings, you can always improve your shot later. Behind the tee line, it's tough to make it better.

5. LEARN HOW TO MISS

At one point or another we're all going to miss shots, so you may as well learn how to miss the right way. Before you attempt a shot, think about the consequences of missing. The scoreboard will dictate the urgency and help clarify the level of risk you should take. If you're up three points, do you need to risk the perfect shot when missing it could set your team back? Instead you could miss the right way—strategically—and be set up for later attempts.

THE DELIVERY

GETTING THE ROCKS TO THE RINGS

"Not on purpose."

—**RANDY FERBEY,** asked by *Off the Record*'s Michael Landsberg if he could duplicate Jeff Stoughton's 360-degree delivery.

WHEN I WAS GROWING UP, my father always pushed me to perfect my delivery technique, stressing things like balance and the position of my feet. Time after time, when all I wanted to do was fire the rock down the ice so it would hit some of the others, he would prod me to keep my back straight and maintain a proper grip on the rock. At the time, these lessons weren't a lot of fun, but in hindsight, I realize that they were a large part of why my delivery is so solid to this day and why I think it's important for

you to pay constant attention to your own delivery technique.

Throwing a rock incorporates balance, strength, timing, and flexibility. Start by placing one foot in the hack (the footrest) closest to the centre line of the ice sheet and holding the rock in the hand closest to the centre line. (Right-handed players place their right foot in the hack and hold the rock with their right hand. Left-handers place their left foot in the hack and hold the rock with their left hand.) The intent is that the rock is always delivered from close to the centre line. In either case, the front foot is equipped with a slider, usually made of Teflon, plastic, or metal; this can be either part of a curling shoe or attached to it by an elastic strap.

In order to learn how to deliver a rock competently, first practise sliding out of the hack without a rock. Place your foot in the hack so that your toes touch the bottom and the ball of your foot rests against the raised back. The free, or slider, foot should be alongside the hack. Crouch down until your knees are fully flexed, keeping your shoulders over your feet. With your non-throwing hand, grasp your broom or a balance device to help maintain your

Keeping your shoulders square is the key to having a consistent delivery and delivering on line. One way to practise is to simply slide out of the hack holding the broom with your fingertips.

balance as you slide out of the hack. If you're using a balance device, it should be alongside the slider foot; if you're using a broom, it should be extended outward, like an outrigger, with the handle snugly above the hip or at the shoulder in front of the arm.

Keeping your trunk relatively horizontal, raise your hips until your legs are almost straight; sweep your slider foot back behind your body, balancing this motion by moving your throwing hand in towards the body and moving your hips back, then sweep your slider leg out and forward while extending your throwing arm. Now push off with the foot in the hack to thrust yourself forward and, essentially, dive forward onto the slider foot, which should be directly behind the throwing arm and centrally under the chest. The hack leg trails behind the body, acting as a rudder to control direction. You'll use your broom or balance device to steady your body during delivery, but the objective is to achieve a slide on the slider foot in balance, with little help from balancing aids.

Your slider foot can be flat on the ice, or, as is common in some parts of Canada, on your toes. While toe sliding—the "tuck" position—enables you to get down low behind the rock, it can be inherently less stable and, since it requires that the knee of the sliding foot be turned well outside the body line, it offers a significant risk of knee injury over time. My father taught me, and I recommend, the flat-foot delivery, where the sole of your foot is flat on the ice and your body is more upright. While you may not get as low as in a tuck, the slide is much more stable and contributes to a solid balance in your delivery. It is also much kinder to your knees as the years pass! In either case, your foot should be turned outwards, at a slight angle to the line of the slide.

It is best that you practise your delivery without a rock until you can slide out past the hog line in a stable and balanced position with your throwing arm extended in front of you. Next comes the delivery with a rock.

At this time, there is another decision to be made: to lift or not to lift. Today, youngsters and new curlers are taught the no-lift delivery. The delivery follows the method outlined above, but at the point where your slider foot is swept back behind your body, the rock is pulled back to just in front of the hack. The rock is then pushed out in front as your hack leg kicks your body out of the hack and the slider foot comes around and under the body directly behind the rock. This requires co-ordination and a certain amount of practice. The need to accelerate 40 pounds of granite in addition to your own weight requires a substantial muscular effort from your hack leg as you kick out of the hack—one disadvantage of the no-lift delivery.

THE BACKSWING DELIVERY

The other option, the one I prefer, is the backswing delivery. In this method, you extend the rock out in front of the hack before your body is raised. As your hips are raised, the rock slides towards the hack and is lifted, allowing it to swing behind the hack as your slider foot swings behind your body. The rock is then swung forward onto the ice as your slider foot comes around to a point beneath the body and behind the rock, and your hack leg kicks out to increase the acceleration of the body and the rock. This method requires less leg effort to get the desired speed out of the hack.

THE WEIGHT

Regardless of your choice of delivery method, the ultimate objective is to deliver a rock at the right speed, or weight, for it to reach its target. There are some curlers, like Mark Nichols, who are known for their uncanny ability to execute with extremely

Always try to be consistent in your weight regardless of the ice conditions.

hard weight, and there are others, like Norway's Dordi Nordby, who are notorious for an exquisitely soft touch. Still others combine the two beautifully.

The rock must be released before the hog line when it is travelling at the ideal speed to execute your shot. The question is when to release to achieve the proper weight. After you kick out of the hack, the rock and your body slow continually according to the amount of friction or resistance. This is the heart of curling: you must decide when you are at the desired speed to release the rock. So, how do you know when to release your rock? It depends on the shot you're trying to make. The various draw shots where the rock stops in, or in front of, the house require that you hold onto the rock longer. You could also slow your kick from the hack. Similarly, the various forms of hits require that the rock be released earlier, while the energy in the rock is higher and it is moving more quickly. You could increase the force of the kick from the hack. And, in the no-lift delivery, your arm is sometimes extended just before release, giving the rock a little more speed.

The weight of a shot affects the curl of the rock. Stones that are thrown with a heavier weight travel faster, so there's less time to bend, or curl. Ice conditions, too, affect the rock, so you may have to adjust the weight of your shots accordingly. But you should always try to be consistent in your weight regardless of the ice conditions. If you tend to throw lightly on a takeout weight, your skip can adjust the broom (target) and give you more or less ice.

Some of the common ways of describing the weight of the shots you may be asked to throw are

Board weight. A shot that has enough force to travel to the back of the sheet.

Draw weight. A shot that stops on the tee line.

Hack weight. A bit less than board weight; the shot has enough force to stop at the hack.

Peel weight. A shot thrown very hard to take out a number of your opponent's rocks.

TO LIFT OR NOT TO LIFT?

THE NO-LIFT DELIVERY is the one most commonly taught to youngsters and beginning curlers today. However, I maintain that there are many advantages to the lift, or backswing, delivery. You create more momentum with the backswing, which means you'll be able to throw the rock much harder and with less effort. You'll probably also find that you're more accurate. I strongly recommend that players begin to experiment with the lift delivery as soon as they are old enough or are comfortable doing so.

➡ THE LIFT DELIVERY

In the address position, take care that your shoulders and knees are facing the target, while the ball of your hack foot is in the back of the hack. Your slider foot should be beside the hack.

Next, press forward slightly to generate momentum.

Lift your hips to initiate the backswing. Swing, but don't lift, the rock straight back, while keeping your weight over your hack foot.

➡ THE LIFT DELIVERY (CONT'D)

Keep your sliding foot well behind the hack. This buys time for the rock to be swung back into position ahead of your sliding foot.

With the backswing delivery, the rock will head towards the target before your sliding foot does.

The rock reaches the ice surface. If this is done properly, your shoulders will be level with the ice, at a 90-degree angle to the target.

As you start to slide down the ice towards the target, most of your weight should be underneath the sternum, on your sliding leg. Your back foot should be stretched out like a rudder.

Keep your throwing arm slightly bent allowing for better feel and more rotation.

The best players keep their shoulders square to the target as they release the rock.

➡ THE NO-LIFT DELIVERY

The address position for the no-lift delivery is identical to the backswing, or lift, delivery: square shoulders, knees facing the target, back of your hack foot in the back of the hack.

Lift your hips to initiate the backward motion, this time sliding the rock along the ice—without lifting it—towards your hack foot.

As you push the stationary rock forward, all your power comes from the hack foot.

The rest of the delivery from this point on is identical to the lift delivery.

This photo illustrates what I consider to be a fault of the no-lift delivery. Compare this picture with the last couple of photos in the lift delivery sequence. Notice how, in this case, the sliding arm is in a very rigid position, causing it to be what I would call overextended. The curler's shoulders are clearly aiming well to the left of the target—you may think you are sliding straight, but you won't ever throw the rock straight if your shoulders aren't square to the target. Invariably, your out-turn will run a little straighter, while your in-turn will curl a little sooner. If you do plan to stick with the no-lift delivery, practise keeping your throwing arm slightly bent. You'll get better results if you do.

starting position

out-turn

in-turn

THE RELEASE (TURN)

The name of the game is "curling." Few rocks will ever travel in a perfectly straight path to your target. Why? The ice is covered with tiny knobs of ice, commonly called "the pebble," which affects the motion of the rock. To control the curl, you turn the rock so that it revolves as it travels, forcing it to curve in the direction of the rotation.

To allow for this, the skip will indicate first where he wants the rock to travel to, or to stop, and then the direction of rotation and the aiming point he believes you need to use. He will then give some form of call or signal indicating the weight, or speed, he wants the rock delivered at. The rest is pretty well up to you.

You make the rock rotate by turning your wrist towards the centre line (an out-turn) or away from it (an in-turn). When rotating the rock, however, it is important to be smooth and gentle, so that no force is exerted that might affect the direction of travel of the rock (you're only setting the rotation of the rock). If you do this, you may be told that you "pushed" or "flipped" the shot, causing it to miss the aiming point.

If you want to throw an in-turn, you should start with the handle of the rock angled slightly away from the centre line. For an out-turn, the handle should be angled slightly towards the centre line. As you come out of the hack, the rock should be directly in front of you at the full extent of your arm. Turn your wrist towards the centre line for an in-turn or away from it for an out-turn. In either case, your elbow and arm should remain straight; only your wrist rotates. You need to cause the rock to rotate only two to four times over the entire length of the ice, and it is essential not to cause it to move off the line to the broom held by the skip.

THE RELEASE

I FIND THAT, regardless of whether I'm throwing the out-turn or the in-turn, I like to grip the handle of the rock the way I would grip a golf club: firmly, but relaxed at the same time. If you golf, you've no doubt been taught to hold the grip of the golf club with your index finger and thumb in a V shape, pointing to your opposite shoulder. This is also a wonderful way to approach the curling grip.

Most curlers tend to throw the in-turn narrow. To correct this, try moving your right thumb farther to the left, or slightly back on the handle at the address position, and you'll avoid the dreaded in-turn wreck on the guard!

➡ THE OUT-TURN

If you're a right-handed curler, as you sit in the hack, look down at the rock in front of you and picture the face of a clock. The open end of the handle will face the 6 o'clock position. To throw the out-turn properly, turn the handle clockwise from 6 to roughly the 8 o'clock position.

As you begin the delivery motion, regardless of whether you use the lift or no-lift delivery, keep the handle at 8 o'clock. As you slide towards the target, nothing changes in your delivery, and nothing changes in your grip.

→ THE OUT-TURN (CONT'D)

As you slide towards the hog line, keep the rock handle at 8 o'clock.

About three or four feet before you release the rock, simply rotate the handle from the 8 o'clock position back to 6. On the follow-through, your hand will look as though you've just finished shaking hands with someone. This simple rotation, from 8 o'clock to 6, will ensure that the counter-clockwise rotation of the rock will be consistent. Ideally, we would like to see roughly three full revolutions as the rock travels down the length of the ice. Too little rotation can cause the rock to curl unnaturally; too much will cause the rock to curl very little.

→ THE IN-TURN

The in-turn release is the exact opposite. Simply turn the handle of the stationary rock from 6 o'clock to the 4 o'clock position, and keep it there throughout your delivery.

The handle of the rock remains at the 4 o'clock position throughout the slide.

Within about three or four feet of releasing the rock, turn the handle clockwise from 4 o'clock to 6, again keeping your hand in a handshake-like position. If this is done properly, the rock will curl clockwise, with roughly three rotations, as it travels to the other end of the sheet.

SLIDING STRAIGHT

I find it amazing how many curlers cannot slide straight towards the broom. Check your footwear and experiment with different shoes until you can slide perfectly straight. The best way to check your slide is to slide, without a rock, straight down the centre line with your throwing arm extended as if you were releasing a rock. When you come to a stop, your throwing arm should be directly on top of the centre line, with no drift to the right or left. Mastering this skill is crucial to becoming a good player.

AIM (HITTING THE BROOM)

Because of the characteristic curve of a curling rock's path, rocks are actually thrown towards a point that is off to one side of the intended target. This target is indicated with the head, or handle, of the skip's broom. Successfully directing the rock to that point is referred to as "hitting the broom."

In order to accurately hit the broom you must aim your body directly at it, aligning yourself so that your shoulders are at a 90-degree angle to the broom. Your shoulders must remain square throughout the slide if you are to hit the broom. Keep your eyes on the target. It is important that your trailing leg be on, or parallel to, the throwing line during the slide and that the trailing foot be also on, or parallel to, the line. A bent trailing leg or foot will have a rudder-like effect on the slide and your body will tend to rotate away from the throwing line.

Similarly, the rock must be on the throwing line, and the turn or rotation put into the rock must be done without causing the rock to veer off course.

Beginners sometimes try to slide up the centre line and then direct the rock at the broom. Trying to change the direction of a 40-pound rock while sliding is complicated by the fact that, to do so, you must overcome the momentum of the rock and your slide. It is crucial that the thrower slide towards the broom, facing it squarely and releasing the rock on that line, with the proper rotation and at the necessary speed. Easy, isn't it?

Determining the aiming point isn't easy, either. The distance between the aiming point and the intended arrival point of the rock is referred to as ice—as in "more ice" or "less ice." When deciding how much ice a shot requires, the skip must take several things into account. While a rock thrown down the same ice at different

A bent trailing leg or foot will have a rudder-like effect on the slide

speeds will tend to curl about the same distance, the speed, or weight, of the rock determines where the rock begins to curl. Consequently, it is essential that the skip communicate the weight to be thrown as well as decide how much ice the shot needs, so that it begins to curl at the appropriate point, then curls the correct amount before travelling to its destination. If a rock curls three feet before coming to rest and you want to hit an opposing rock with enough force to remove it, then a properly thrown rock will have curled much less than three feet when it gets to the opposing rock.

The skip must also think about ice conditions. If the ice has imperfections (runs) in particular areas, these must be considered. In addition, the act of sweeping near the rock can affect the distance it will travel.

TRAINING WHEELS

I developed this drill for my kids. By the age of five, both of my children had developed tremendous balance and great technique without the fear of falling. If you wanted me to make you a better curler in a hurry, we'd spend the first three days doing this drill.

Curlers who don't learn a balanced delivery will tend to use the rock for balance, making it nearly impossible to hit the broom on a consistent basis. The "training wheels" drill is a simple and effective way to improve your delivery. Slide out of the hack in the delivery position, holding your broom on the ice with both hands. By keeping your hands on the broom, you eliminate an imbalance in your body position. This drill keeps your shoulders square, your head and shoulders up high, your back end low, and your sliding foot right beneath your sternum for perfect balance. All this, while removing the fear of falling—thus the name "training wheels." Fight the temptation to throw rocks until you have mastered this drill.

DRILLS

The best way to improve your game is to throw a lot of rocks and practise actual curling shots. The following eight drills are simple to set up and easy to score so that you can track your progress. They can be completed by one player, two players, two against two, or by a full team if you want to practise sweeping and sweeping judgment.

DRILL 1: STRAIGHT BACKS ON THE CENTRE LINE
Develops release and weight control

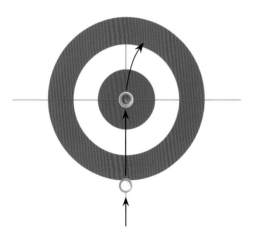

Simply set up a rock on the button and place a guard directly in front of it on the centre line, touching the rings, leaving yourself a straight six-foot runback. To score a point, the guard has to make contact with the rock on the button. Eight shots are thrown—four in-turns and four out-turns—for a maximum score of eight points.

TIP: Teammates should throw the same weight during this drill (board to normal weight.)

Variation: Straight Backs on the Eight-Foot

For this variation, set up a rock on the middle of the eight-foot (on the tee line) and place a guard six feet directly in front of it, leaving yourself a straight six-foot runback. Proceed as above.

DRILL 2: ANGLE RAISE
Improves aim and understanding of angles

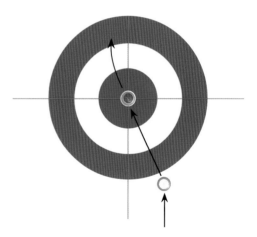

You have to know where to hit to be successful. Set up a rock on the button, with a corner guard six feet in front of the tee line and two to three feet to the left of the centre line, leaving yourself roughly a six-foot angle raise. To score a point, the guard has to make contact with the rock on the button. Eight shots are thrown—four in-turns and four out-turns—for a maximum score of eight points.

TIP: This is good practice for your up-weight shots.

Variation: Opposite Angle Raise

Same procedure as above, but place the corner guard two to three feet to the right of the centre line.

DRILL 3: HIT AND STAY
Improves balance, alignment, and weight control

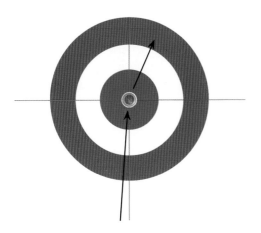

Set up a rock on the button. To score a point, you have to hit and stay with your shooter, staying in the four-foot. Throw eight shots (board to normal weight)—four

in-turns and four out-turns—for a maximum score of eight points.

TIP: Controlling your weight will make this drill easier.

Variation: Hit and Stay in the 12-Foot

Set up a rock on the tee line in the middle of the 12-foot. To score your point, the shooter has to stay in the 12-foot circle only.

DRILL 4: HIT AND ROLL TO THE FOUR-FOOT
Helps to throw the proper weight for a shot

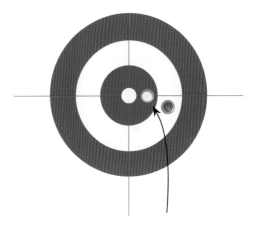

Place a rock two feet in front of the tee line, at the middle of the eight-foot—on the right-hand side of the rings. The object is to hit the rock and roll to the four-foot. The stationary rock does not have to be removed from the rings. To score your point, the shooter has to stay in the four-foot. Throw eight shots—four in-turns and four out-turns—for a maximum score of eight points.

TIP: You'll have more success with this shot with soft weight. Throw this one to the sweepers.

Variation: Opposite Hit and Roll to the Four-Foot

Same procedure as above, but place the target rock on the left-hand side of the rings.

DRILL 5: DRAW SHOTS
Helps weight control

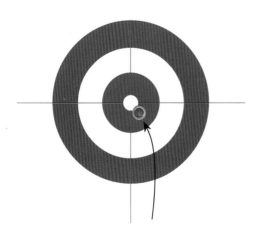

You can't be a good skip until you can draw the four-foot under pressure. Simply draw to the four-foot for your point. Sixteen shots are thrown—eight in-turns and eight out-turns—for a maximum of 16 points.

TIP: Remember to take each rock out of play before the next draw shot.

DRILL 6: ZONE DRAW DRILL
Develops weight control

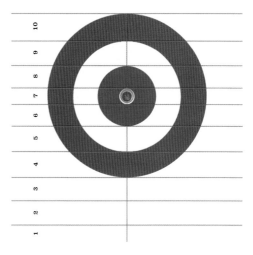

People tend to practise the draw to the four-foot, but you have to be able to position rocks all over the sheet, especially the closer zones. Using the zone system of your choice, randomly pick a zone for your target. Score one point for every draw that stops in the proper zone. Throw 16 shots—eight in-turns, eight out-turns—for a maximum score of 16 points.

TIP: Coaches, this drill can help the lead practise 1, 2, and 3 zone guards.

DRILL 7: HIT AND STAY DRILL
Improves ice-reading skills and control

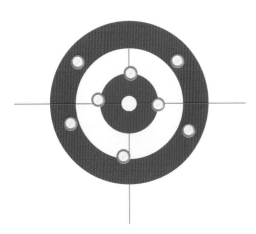

Throw all eight yellow rocks into any part of the rings. Then try to remove all the yellow rocks while leaving the red rocks in the rings. Score one point for each success-ful draw to the rings, and one point for each rock that remains in the rings when the end is over. Maximum score is 16 points (all yellow rocks are out of the rings with all the red rocks remaining).

TIP: Don't just draw your opening eight rocks towards the button—spread them out! It's tougher to get your draw weight, but much easier to hit and stay with your last eight rocks if the draws have been spread out.

DRILL 8: REVERSE FERBEY DRILL
Helps sweeping judgment

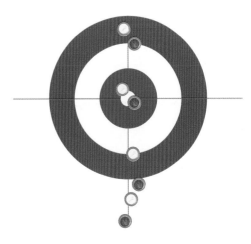

The goal of this drill is to get as many rocks in play as possible. Simply draw the first rock towards the centre line, as deep as possible without going through the rings. Continue this pattern with only one rule: every rock you throw has to be shorter in distance than the previous one, without touching the previous rock. In other words, stack the rocks. Continue this drill until you can't fit any more rocks over the hog line! If you throw one rock too deep, the drill is over. Score one point for each rock made, to a maximum of 16.

TIP: When performed with sweepers, this drill teaches them not to oversweep.

③
SWEEPING
KEEPING IT CLEAN

> "I would rather have a lead who is an average shot maker and a tremendous sweeper than the other way around."
> —RUSS HOWARD

SWEEPING IS PERHAPS the most underrated and underappreciated part of curling. I am still amazed that some teams are willing to regularly forfeit three to four points in games because of poor sweeping. The art of sweeping is seen by many curlers as less important than the ability to make shots, but the two elements are inseparable. Sweeping can make the difference between squeezing a rock past the guard and executing a triple takeout or rubbing on the guard and having to give up three.

Sweeping serves several purposes. Obviously, it removes any debris from in front of the rock. It doesn't take much effort to do this, and you will hear skips asking sweepers to "clean, just clean" on a shot that is looking good. More importantly, sweeping can make a rock slide farther or curl slightly less. Two good sweepers can create enough pressure to warm the ice slightly creating a thin film of water that reduces friction and makes it easier for the rock to slide. It follows a straighter path because the rock gets to its target sooner and has less time to curl.

Since the early 1980s, brushes have replaced the brooms. Newer brushes have lightweight carbon-fibre handles, while interchangeable fabric-covered heads are available for different ice surfaces. A good horsehair head can supposedly cut through frost better than a synthetic head, but frost isn't an issue in most curling clubs. One of the great innovations in sweeping over the past few decades has been the invention of the swivel head, which allows sweepers to adjust their brooms to the angle that suits them best.

There are a variety of handles, made from wood, graphite, or plastic. The biggest difference between them is weight. This may not seem like a big deal when you're playing only once or twice a week, but the effect that a lighter curling broom can have on your game when you're involved in a week-long tournament, where you may be expected to play four or five games over two days, is immeasurable.

HOLDING THE BROOM

I believe that there are three major differences that separate average sweepers from elite sweepers: the position of the hands, foot positioning, and the distribution of weight over the broom. As with most

aspects of curling, the differences in sweeping technique between average and elite curlers may seem small, but the end result is often huge.

New curlers almost always make the mistake of getting too low on the broom. I understand that the reason for doing this is to get better leverage, but the act is counterproductive. If you take a look at the really good sweepers—Marcel Rocque and Scott Pfeiffer, front end for the Ferbey team for example—you'll see that they keep their top hand close to the end of the broom and their bottom hand roughly halfway down the handle in a comfortable position. Being too low on the broom plays havoc with your line of sight and makes it more difficult to judge the speed of the rock, not to mention that it can result in a chiropractic nightmare for your back.

The idea is to create as much downward pressure and speed as possible with your brush in order to create the maximum amount of friction.

Sweep directly in front of the rock and as close as possible to it. If you are sweeping to one side of the rock, you risk pushing debris in front of it. Move your broom across the entire running surface of the rock, but don't sweep beyond its path, or your sweeping will be less effective.

HOLDING THE BRUSH

The wrong way to sweep. Note the broom head running in line with the path of the rock. This leaves gaps in the intended direction of the rock.

The correct way to sweep. Note that the broom is twisted at a right angle to the intended direction of the rock. This way, part of the broom is always in front of the rock.

Snowplowing—placing the handle of the broom directly over the moving rock, moving your broom head in the same direction as the rock—is illegal.

Your lower hand should be roughly one foot from the head of the broom.

This way, your weight will still be forward on your left foot, but you'll have your left hand lower, squaring up your lower back.

The same reasoning applies if you're sweeping on the right-hand side of the rock. Here, the sweeper's right foot is forward, with the left hand low—again, it's hard on the back.

With your right foot forward and your right hand low, your lower-back muscles don't have to work as hard.

If you're sweeping on the left side of the rock, your body weight is forward on your front foot—in this case, your left. Keeping your right arm low gives you a better view of the target, but I find it very taxing on the lower back.

FOOTWORK

If you're like me, developing the footwork involved in sweeping will take hard work and patience. But the effort will pay off, because footwork is, without a doubt, the key to successful sweeping. You can sweep either with grippers on both your shoes, or in a push-slide method with a gripper on your back foot.

When wearing grippers on both feet, keep your body weight on the balls of your feet and continue down the ice in a quick stepping motion, bringing your back foot to the front foot, then stepping forward again with your front foot.

For the push-slide method, bend your knees slightly and keep as much weight as possible balanced over your front foot (the sliding leg) while pushing with your gripper foot (your back leg). Your gripper foot pushes your body as you move down the sheet—pushing, then coming up to the slider foot and pushing again. Your sliding foot should be pointed in the direction your body is moving; your gripper foot is your rudder/balance point, and you glide on the slider.

When wearing the gripper, keep your weight on the balls of your feet as you balance on the front leg, which should be kept bent at all times.

Continue down the ice in a quick stepping motion, with your back foot coming to the front foot, then pushing off.

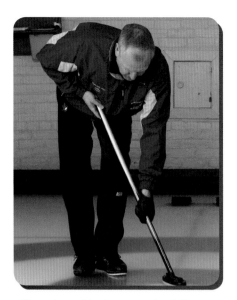

When using a slider, keep as much weight as possible balanced over your front, or sliding, leg, with a definite bend to your knee.

Push with your gripper foot and use it as a rudder or balance point while you glide on the slider.

SWEEPING WITH A PARTNER

Our Olympic team faced an interesting situation. I was asked to skip the team, which meant I would hold the broom for six rocks, as all skips do; but I was also asked to throw the second rocks in the rotation. Brad, the fourth thrower, held the broom for my shots and was the sweeper for the other four shots of the end. This allowed a much younger Brad Gushue to sweep, while I was able to hold the broom and call the strategy for the maximum six shots. You can set up your team in any fashion you like, but there are two things to remember: each player on the team throws two consecutive rocks; and, barring injury, the lineup for sweeping and holding the broom in the first end has to be maintained throughout the entire game.

Ideally you want one sweeper on either side of the rock for the most effective results. There are two reasons for this. One, it is easier to keep both brushes closer to the rock, creating maximum effectiveness. Two, if the rock is curling to the right, have your inside sweeper (closest to the rock) positioned on the right side of the rock. Tests have shown that the sweeper's away stroke is much more effective than the inward motion, so in this example it can help to minimize the curl. If you want more curl, have your sweepers switch, with your inside sweeper on the left side of the rock. Both sweepers are responsible for the weight of the rock.

A lot of curlers think it's the skip's job to get the shot in the right place, but in fact it's everyone's responsibility, including the sweepers'. The sweepers assess where the rock is likely to stop, and communicate that information to the player in the house. The player in the house has the final say on the path of the rock (line) and will direct the sweepers when to sweep "for line." The top teams in the world are the ones best at this communication. It is the sweepers' job to concentrate on the weight of the rock, taking into consideration the path the rock is travelling on, the amount of rotation in the rock, and which rock is being swept (is it a fast rock? a cutter?).

With two sweepers on the same side of the rock, footwork becomes a problem. The second sweeper must stand about three or four feet away from the running surface of the rock.

When the sweepers are positioned on either side of the rock, both can get as close to the rock as possible, thus allowing them to work more effectively.

SWEEPING WITH A PARTNER

IN ORDER TO BE EFFECTIVE, the two sweepers need to communicate and to co-ordinate their footwork. Equally important is proper positioning. Most club curlers that I have seen stand at the hog line while they wait for the thrower to release the rock. The problem is that, by the time the two sweepers catch up to the rock and are in a balanced position, ready to sweep (don't forget you're on ice!), the rock is almost halfway down the sheet. This is especially likely to be the case on a takeout.

Sweepers should be positioned, ready to sweep, off to the side of the sheet—which gives the thrower ample room to deliver the rock—and at the back line, which allows the two sweepers time to get up to the speed of the shot being thrown.

As the thrower starts to deliver the rock, the sweepers start to move at the appropriate speed.

Notice the sweepers starting to get closer to the rock, always conscious of the thrower's broom.

As the thrower gets ready to release the rock, the sweepers are up to speed, still angling in towards the released rock.

As the stone is released, the sweepers are ready—in this particular case, in a take-out—well before the hog line.

Timing rocks with a stopwatch. Many curlers use a stopwatch to anticipate how far a rock will travel by timing how fast a delivered rock travels from the backline to the first hog line. On good ice, every one-tenth of a second represents about six feet of ice. In this example, a thrower's draw to the button crossed the hog line in 3.7 seconds. The numbers superimposed on this photo show how you can estimate how a heavier or lighter shot will end up, based on the split time. The lower the number, the faster the speed of the rock and the farther it will travel.

USING A STOPWATCH

Most young teams nowadays are taught to use a stopwatch to help judge where a draw shot will end up. The idea is that, by timing how long it takes the rock to cover a small portion of the sheet (from the back line to the first hog line), sweepers can gauge how far the rock will travel, and therefore how much or how little sweeping is needed.

Let's say the "split time" on a draw to the button is 3.6 seconds. If a rock crosses the first hog line in 3.5, it is obviously travelling faster and will slide past the button. Each tenth of a second equates to roughly six feet of travel.

Unfortunately, a stopwatch doesn't take into consideration who threw the rock. Some curlers glide farther than others, a

One of the first things I suggested to the Gushue team was to throw away the stopwatch and simply watch the rocks and the ice.

factor that can distort your split time. Nor can a stopwatch evaluate which rock has been thrown and which path the rock will follow down the ice, which can also distort your split time. My greatest concern about using a stopwatch is that it's so similar to teaching students how to do multiplication with calculators: unless they learn to multiply without the help of calculators, they won't learn the underlying concepts. Once the rock is past the first hog line, you are not relying on the stopwatch anyway. It's all about concentration.

One of the first things I suggested to the Gushue team was to throw away the stopwatch and simply watch the rocks and the ice. An expert sweeper has to have the technique while paying constant atten-

KEEPING A CLEAR BRUSH HEAD

SYNTHETIC BRUSHES (which I think are the most effective) lose a lot of their effectiveness if they are not cleaned on a regular basis. A small fingernail brush is ideal for cleaning the brush heads. But be careful: I see so many teams that faithfully clean their brushes after virtually every shot, then leave the debris right where they are standing on the sheet of ice— this is like shooting yourself in the foot! And don't clean your brush over the carpet, either, or the debris will be tracked back onto the ice. Instead, clean your brush over a garbage receptacle at the end of the ice. With hair brooms, check the heads frequently to ensure that loose hairs are removed.

tion to where the rock is going. In a very short time, Mark Nichols, Jamie Korab, and Brad Gushue were able to judge speed more accurately without a stopwatch, and their ability to put the rocks in the right spots was a huge reason for our success at the Olympics.

BE PREPARED

CREATING A GAME PLAN

"Even though circumstances may cause interruptions and delays, never lose sight of your goal. Instead, prepare yourself in every way you can by increasing your knowledge and adding to your experience, so that you can make the most of opportunity when it occurs."

—MARIO ANDRETTI, Formula One driver

PERHAPS THE SINGLE MOST important factor in our team winning the Olympic trials and the gold medal at the 2006 Winter Olympics was the creation of a game plan in the summer and early fall of 2005.

After their successful attempt at qualifying for the trials, the Brad Gushue rink participated in the 2005 Brier, representing their home province of Newfoundland and Labrador. They did not perform as well as they had expected. Knowing they would face an

incredibly difficult field at the Olympic trials the following November, they sat down with their coach, Toby McDonald, and asked him a very simple question: "Are we good enough to win the trials and make it to the Olympics?" Coach McDonald bluntly said no, and in my opinion he deserves full credit for his honesty.

In response to the obvious need to improve quickly, Coach McDonald then organized and chaired a number of meetings aimed at creating a blueprint that would define and document the team's goals and objectives for the season.

The game plan looked at a host of issues, including team and individual goals, assessment and evaluation, style of play, sweeping, conditioning, strategy, and mental toughness.

Now, you have to remember that I'm from the old school of curling, where you pick up your broom in September or October and head to the rink, ready to start play in a local league in preparation for upcoming bonspiels and the provincial playdowns—usually held in February. I had very rarely, if ever, participated in a brainstorming session in the off-season. A decade or two ago, I might have dismissed outright the idea of taking part in such a series of meetings. As unaccustomed as I was to the idea, it didn't take long for me to realize how invaluable these encounters would be as we began our journey through an improbable Olympic season.

Looking back, I remember that some topics demanded more discussion and debate than others. While it seemed relatively easy to find common ground on issues such as long-term team goals, coming to agreement on others—such as team practice, playing time, and style of play—took a bit longer.

Whether you are a novice, competitive, or Olympic curler, it is vital to your success—and the success of your team—that you sit down before the season begins and create a game plan.

PERSONAL GOALS

In defining personal goals, you are basically asking each team member to come up with a number of goals that he or she wishes to achieve, whether by the end of the season or in the longer term. The goal may be as simple as trying to stay healthy for the entire season, or as complex as trying to accumulate a draw or peel percentage of 85 to 90 per cent. Accordingly, as we'll see in a moment, these objectives must be backed up with strategies that will help accomplish them.

During our meeting in St. John's, we simply went around the table and asked the guys to throw out some ideas. Naturally, the lads were a little tentative at first. But as soon as we started to loosen up and have some fun with the exchange, a number of really good objectives came to the forefront. Of course, depending on where you play in the lineup, your goals are bound to be somewhat different from those of everybody else on the team.

For example, Jamie Korab and Mike

Competitive curlers should focus on more complex issues like learning how to miss the right way.

Adam, our front end, were adamant that by the end of the season they would become one of the best front ends in Canada. Jamie and Mike are strong front-end players, but they felt their sweeping judgment could improve. We developed some drills that would enable them to do so.

Mark Nichols, one of the hardest-throwing thirds in the world, recognized the need to develop a finesse game. Meanwhile, Brad Gushue worked with a sport psychologist in the area of mental toughness. Obviously, you can do only so much, especially in one season. Trying to improve every facet of your game is impossible and even counterproductive. There is one very important rule of thumb that you need to keep in mind when putting together your list of goals: you need to be realistic.

Any goal, whether long- or short-term, team or individual, needs to be attainable. If you're a novice and your goal is to be in the 95th percentile in every shot-making category, you're probably setting yourself up for failure. If you're a baseball player and your lifetime batting average is .125, you're probably not going to challenge Ted Williams' .406 mark in one season. Defining personal goals is beneficial only if you can realistically hope to achieve them.

WHAT DO YOU WANT TO ACHIEVE?

If you're a novice curler who is just beginning to play the game, or if you have been playing once or twice a month at the local club level, look at improving your technique over the course of the season. Set a goal to practise until you have mastered your delivery and sweeping techniques, and keep in mind that no matter what level you compete at, curling takes skill. Perhaps you might want to take a look at getting an extra hour or two on the ice to practise. Without a doubt, every hour you can get at the rink will improve your game.

Competitive curlers should focus on more complex issues like learning how to miss the right way. For example, a draw that is a couple of feet light of its intended target is better than one that is a couple of feet heavy—the lighter draw has the potential to be raised into position, while the one that slides behind the tee line can be detrimental to you if the opposition freezes to it.

One thing I definitely believe should be on any competitive curler's list of long-term goals is to improve their shot percentage on a consistent basis. I have never been a great fan of percentages, but there are ways to evaluate your game that can improve your level of play. I would tell coaches that I'd prefer to see emphasis put less on the individual's percentage than on an accurate assessment of the shots that have been missed. For example, if a competitive curler has a shooting percentage of 80 per cent, focus on the 20 per cent of shots that

were missed—and how they were missed. I guarantee you there will be a pattern. If there are five missed out-turn shots, record how they were missed. Were they consistently wide and heavy? Chances are that that a curler who misses an in-turn shot will miss it narrow. Now the coach has a golden opportunity to work with the player on addressing how the shots were missed. The skip, too, may simply remember when indicating the target with his broom to tighten the ice up on the out-turn and give a little extra ice on the in-turn for that particular curler.

WHAT AM I PREPARED TO DO TO GET THERE?

After you have established some personal goals, you need to back them up with a strategy to achieve them.

You to add something new to your routine. For example, if one of your personal goals is to enjoy an injury-free season, then you might need to look at adding strength, conditioning, and nutritional segments to your off-ice routine.

You might need to be willing to sacrifice one part of your game in order to strengthen another. If you have been a hitting specialist in the past, but recognize that your team has squandered scoring opportunities

PERSONAL GOALS:
RUSS HOWARD, 2005–2006

1) Strengthen my sliding knee and have professional assessment and advice as to appropriate exercises
2) Improve flexibility
3) Strengthen my lower back
4) Improve my peel weight for consistency and accuracy

because of your inability to play a finesse game, you might need to add whole sessions where you practise nothing but freeze and draw shots in an all-out blitz to make this a better part of your game.

TEAM GOALS

Once the members of your team have established some personal goals, it is time to come together and determine the goals and objectives of your team as a whole. Again, reality needs to be your compass as you decide on where your team wants to be at the end of the season and in future years.

Your long-term team goals are extremely important. While it may be acceptable, and actually unavoidable, that long-term

TEAM GOALS:
TEAM GUSHUE, 2005–2006

1) Improve shot making

2) Achieve better fitness

3) Improve ice-reading skills

4) Improve strategy

5) Gain experience

personal goals will vary from one individual to the next, everyone on the team, from the coach on down, must be on the same page when it comes to your team goals.

Whether your team is getting together once or twice a month for some recreational curling or fighting for a spot in a national championship, it is crucial to team harmony, and to the enjoyment of the game by all, that everyone on the team be aware of, and agree on, the team's ultimate objectives.

WHERE DO WE WANT TO GO/WHEN DO WE WANT TO GET THERE?

If your team is just beginning to play together and simply wants to play once a week for the exercise and enjoyment of the sport, then a sensible and legitimate objective is simply to have some fun together and get to know and understand the game a bit better by the time spring rolls around.

If you're a novice team that is ambitious and wishes someday to step it up a notch and become a competitive curling team, you should consider a four- or five-year plan that details your intention to increase practice and playing time so that you will, in five years' time, be in a position to compete with provincial-level rinks.

This blueprint will capture your team's intent to do what it takes to increase your skill and fitness level in order to take your team to that next level. There is nothing that binds your team to being at the novice level for eternity. If your squad has desire, enthusiasm, and the ability to do what it takes to get better, there is nothing stopping you from reaching more ambitious goals further down the road.

If your team believes it can compete at the provincial or national level, your goals obviously need to be more challenging. Your team may feel that it has a legitimate shot at winning some coin, or even capturing a provincial or national championship. If that is the case, don't be afraid to make that your long-term goal. But be prepared to make the sacrifices that teams with these goals need to make.

It's crucial for team members to be on the same page here. If the skip is eager to compete for a provincial championship, but the lead and second have a work or home schedule that doesn't allow them to play more than once or twice a month, the team goal will simply not be met. In such a case, and it is really quite common, one of two things needs to happen: either the players part ways, or the team lowers its expectations.

My suggestion for any competitive team is to shoot high and not leave any regrets on the table. If February comes and you've given it your all and you end up not winning that championship, then at least you know you did your best.

PRACTICE TIME

I've always felt that practice time is a matter of individual preference. Some players love to be at the rink every day, fine-tuning their game, throwing rock after rock, hoping to find that perfect draw weight—or spending hours poring over video, hoping to find their opponent's fatal flaw. Others don't like the idea of spending hours practising and actually find it counterproductive to their game. Personally, I'm probably somewhere in between. I don't believe there is a right or wrong answer here; ultimately, it boils down to the long-term personal goals the members of your team have established, as well as a regular assessment of your performance.

If your long-term personal goal is to hit as well as Kevin Martin or sweep as well as Marcel Rocque or Marcia Gudereit, then you're going to have to get to the rink on a regular basis and do the drills. If you're setting such a heavy goal for yourself, appropriate practice time is a must.

Lee Trevino, a legendary golf pro, was asked what the difference was between a professional golfer and a good amateur. His response: "About 400,000 golf balls."

If you are keeping detailed assessments of your play and notice that your takeout percentage has dipped into the 60th or 70th percentile, then you should probably consider increasing your practice time and getting that part of your game back to where it was. On the other hand, if you're playing well, staying with the status quo might be prudent. Why fix something that isn't broken? Practice time is about feel, and you'll probably have to adjust a few times throughout the season.

There will be a noticeable difference in the way the rocks and ice react on club ice as opposed to arena ice. If you are gearing up for your important event, try to find the practice situation that emulates the conditions you will be playing on at that event. For example, if you are going to a competition where the rocks have tremendous curl, try to find a curling club in your area that offers similar conditions.

One thing I think you should keep in mind about your practice sessions is that they can really cause friction among teammates. I am a stickler for making and keeping a commitment to practice and staying in shape for the entire year, and a number of years ago I had a teammate who was not willing to spend the necessary hours at the rink and the gym. I felt it was important to be honest with him and let him know that I felt our team deserved a better commitment. In the weeks and months following our discussion, his commitment level rose somewhat, but it remained a bone of contention for the entire season. It is very important to make obligations known at the very beginning and stick to them. Differences in preparation techniques and practice preferences will exist—they just have to be brought out into the open in team discussion.

For novice curlers, it is probably not wise to contemplate spending all your time curling. In a practice session, you can spend half an hour throwing 50 rocks, as opposed to a only 16 during a two-hour game. Practice time allows you to focus on particular shots that you've identified as weak areas in your game. Lee Trevino, a legendary golf pro, was asked what the difference was between a professional golfer and a good amateur. His response: "About 400,000 golf balls."

Be slow but sure, and plan on spending two or three hours a week at the rink or gym in addition to your weekend matches. The next year, if you wish, increase those practice hours so that your improvement will be gradual but steady.

Competitive curlers also need to spend time at the rink in addition to the time they spend playing in tournaments. At this point, I want to give you perhaps the most important piece of advice I can: become a student of the game. While you're spending this time at the rink, don't just concentrate on the skills and strategies that your position demands; branch out and learn about as many aspects of the game that you can. If you're a lead, observe your skip and those of other clubs and watch how they manage a game or handle adversity. This philosophy applies to everyone. If you take the time to become a student of the game, and not just a master of your position, you'll become an invaluable member of each and every team you play for in your career.

PLAYING TIME/TRAVELLING TIME

When I was approached to play with the Gushue rink, time was the one area that caused me the most apprehension. Understanding that the team was setting its sights on the Olympics, I just didn't know whether I could give enough of myself to the squad to be as effective and as valuable as I knew I wanted to be. To give you an idea of the degree of the time commitment, it might be best to take a look at the kind of schedule a few of my competitors were booking.

My brother Glenn was planning to play on 10 of the 11 weekends leading up to the Olympic trials. He travelled across North America in the months leading up to the national selection tournament and saw that workload as a burden he was willing to undertake. Randy Ferbey had a very similar approach; from the moment he won the World Curling Championships in Victoria, B.C., in 2005, he was on a mission. He felt that he had to devote all his time and effort to winning the Olympic trials in Halifax.

Since I was the fifth man, I committed to two of the 11 weekends with the Gushue team before the trials. I was already curling in six other events with my New Brunswick team, so I was getting plenty of games in preparation for the trials. My role at this point was to observe the team and provide any necessary input.

If you're a beginner, it is certainly not necessary to take in every bonspiel. If you can play one or two nights a week, you will be more than able to meet all of your personal goals, and the sport will remain enjoyable. If you're a competitive curler, then of course you'll need to commit to a schedule that allows you to quickly get into—and stay in—midseason form. Whether it was for Team Ontario or Team New Brunswick, I liked the idea of playing in at least two or three cashspiels a month and throwing practice rocks three or four times a week.

FINANCIAL COMMITMENT

Everyone has limits. In order to properly gauge where you can go with this sport, you need to determine your financial limits.

Curling is generally not an expensive sport. If you head down to your local curling club, they can get you started with everything you need. Once you've been outfitted with shoes, a broom, and maybe some gloves, and paid the membership fee for one of your local club's leagues, you're pretty much ready to start. But unless you have an outstanding sponsor helping you with expenses, curling competitively can

become very expensive. Depending on which part of the country you live in, travel expenses for flights, hotels, meals, and entry fees can eat up a large part of your annual budget. One of the criteria my teams have always looked at is the prize money for qualifying teams. If we didn't feel we could qualify for the final eight and at least break even, we would really have to think twice about attending the spiel. Of course, it always helps the bottom line if you can win a tournament or two and take home $10,000 or more in prize money.

The sport of curling has been blessed with a significant number of great sponsors over the last couple of years. The success of the junior, women's, men's, and senior curling teams at the national, international, and Olympic levels would not be possible without the assistance of our sponsors. Our sport has been able to grow both in popularity and stature because of them.

My advice is to remember, each and every time you and your team take to the ice, that you represent not only yourself and your team, but also your sponsors. Do your best to represent your sponsors with pride and class, and remember to thank them for their help and support at the end of the season.

The competitive curler needs to look at everything from accommodations when travelling at home or abroad to equipment repair and replacement. If your goal is to win a provincial championship, you can probably count on $10,000–$20,000 or more in expenses for a season.

ASSESSMENT AND EVALUATION

If your aim is to become a better curler, a winning curler, then a regular assessment and evaluation of your game is a must. Whether you are a novice or a competitive curler, an honest appraisal of where you are is crucial. Assessment and evaluation can be done both formally and informally, and it should come from a number of sources.

The key ingredients to valuable assessment are honesty and constructiveness. If you are not willing to be honest with yourself or your teammates when offering assessment and evaluation, then their worth is minimal. You need to be willing and able to look at each and every segment of your game, recognize what needs to be improved, and be willing to take guidance and advice without becoming defensive. This leads me to the second key ingredient: constructiveness. There is a huge difference between constructive criticism, destructive criticism, and sarcasm. If you are delivering advice and tips to your teammates or coaches, make sure it is done in a positive

and uplifting way. If your criticism is given in a negative or demeaning manner, it may cause irreparable damage to team chemistry.

There is no better example of valuable assessment and honesty than what happened to Mark Nichols at the 2006 Winter Olympics in Torino, Italy. Mark struggled to meet his high standards during the week, after following a suggestion from a support staff member that caused him to become slightly erratic on his hits. Mark, being a team player, kept his frustration inside most of the week, until the round robin was over. We had one practice before the sudden-death semifinal against the United States, and Mark, disgusted with his shot making during the session, walked off the ice with five minutes left in practice. I noticed his frustration, so I went to Toby, our coach, and requested that we schedule an extra practice instead of accepting hockey tickets. Toby agreed with this suggestion and relayed it to Jim Waite, our national coach, who managed to set up additional practice time in the rink next door. I held the broom for Mark while Toby and Brad observed. After some more errant shots, I simply suggested to Mark that he was doing something slightly different from the way he had been throwing at the Olympic trials in Halifax, and I asked what he thought it was. He responded that he had stopped pushing the rock on his release. Being the brain surgeon that I am, I suggested that Mark try pushing it again. Voilà! One or two attempts later, Mark ran off seven consecutive raised takeouts and, because of his valuable assessment of himself and his honesty with the team, came up with two of the greatest curling performances (at the most opportune time) in Canadian curling history.

SELF-ASSESSMENT

There are some curlers who assess their own performances each and every time they are on the ice. Whether it is during an informal throw at the local club or in the final ends of a skins game, they are constantly paying attention to what they are doing and using their insights to help themselves to improve.

I'm not saying that everyone needs to scrutinize their game to this degree, but regular self-assessment can be a valuable part of the equation as you move towards becoming a better curler.

There are two types of self-assessment: informal and formal. Informal self-assessment is done on the spot, and usually without the help of statistics or percentages.

Let's say, for example, that you noticed that incorrect weight distribution coming out of the hack caused you to wobble during the delivery of your last rock. In this case, recognizing the problem instantly can promote an immediate correction. This is informal self-assessment in action.

A formal self-assessment is something that you are perhaps more familiar with. Formal self-assessments are done with the help of stats that teams accumulate and document; these numbers can be used by players as a reference, whether in practice, during a game, or at some later point when they can take the appropriate time to digest the information and use it to improve their game.

Remember, one of my favourite lines is "Percentages are for losers." It's not the 80 per cent shots that you make, it's the 20 per cent that you miss and why. Look for the patterns. Is the out-turn usually wide? Recognizing such patterns will instantaneously improve your game. Either the player can make adjustments, or the skip can adjust the ice accordingly. One way or the other, the team will improve its shot-making abilities. Another factor that a team needs to record and monitor is how the shots are being missed—that is, was the shot overthrown on the out-turn, or under-thrown? I bet you'll see a pattern. Make the adjustments and improve the results.

Don't forget to assess the ice at these times also. That way, you learn to recognize differences and changes in the ice surface(s) and compensate accordingly.

TEAM ASSESSMENT

While self-assessment is a task you personally take on, team assessment involves each team member—and a coach, if this applies—and demands a much more open and co-operative environment.

At times, we are too close to our performance to get a realistic take on where we are and where we need to be. That is why it's so helpful to have others willing and able to give us constructive advice and guidance. As with self-assessment, team assessment can take on different shapes and forms. It may be something performed simply and quickly during a game or practice, or it may also be done more formally at a later date.

Perhaps a teammate notices some quirk in your delivery, or a change in the ice or in the behaviour of a particular rock, and relays the information during a timeout. This is a great example of team assessment taking place while the game is in progress. A one-on-one with the coach behind closed doors after the season is also a model of

team assessment, but one that is much more deliberate. In either case, the help can be invaluable, and it makes everyone responsible for each other.

As I mentioned earlier, the biggest factor with team assessment is the spirit in which it is given. If team assessment is done in a positive and constructive way, it will almost always be accepted graciously and acted upon immediately. If, on the other hand, it is done sarcastically in the heat of the moment, it can cause immense damage to team chemistry.

SCOUTING

Since few teams have the luxury of sending advance scouts to arenas across North America with the sole purpose of detailing opponents' strengths and weaknesses, we often have to do our own scouting.

If your team is lucky enough to have a coach or a fifth, scouting can become one of his or her responsibilities. During events, the coach can keep one eye on the strengths, weaknesses, and preferences of potential opponents. If you don't have a coach, you can do most of the scouting yourself. If your game ends early and other teams are still playing, why not head to the stands and take in an end or two before heading home? You might be surprised at how much information you can pick up simply by becoming a spectator.

If your team isn't in the first draw or first practice, it can also benefit from scouting the ice you are to play on. This can provide valuable information which can be tested and/or confirmed in the practice. (Practice should be structured and preplanned.)

STYLES OF PLAY
PLAYING TO YOUR TEAM'S STRENGTHS

Every player and team has strengths and weaknesses. It's important to be aware of what your strong points and vulnerabilities are. I am a big believer in the theory that you construct a game plan so that you play to your strengths first and your opponent's weaknesses second.

If your team's strength is in hitting—and especially if you have a skip or third who loves to throw the big weight—then positioning rocks in front of the opponent's counters early in the end is always beneficial. Conversely, if you are a draw team, having the front end throwing long guards promotes a finesse game later on in the end.

In the 2003 Scott Tournament of Hearts, Colleen Jones was down one or two points early in the game. Colleen played a very defensive style, despite the fact that she needed to score points. The television crew continually criticized her conservative approach, arguing that the scoreboard dictated otherwise. What the commentators didn't realize was that this was Team Jones's game plan, and they were the best in the world at it. If you remember correctly, Colleen's opposition left her with a decision that would win or lose the Canadian championship. Her choice was between drawing the eight-foot on good ice, with good sweepers, or throwing a hit and staying on a rock on the side of the eight-foot—with no room for error on the wide side of the shot. Again, the commentators could not believe the decision to hit, thinking it was the more difficult of the two shots; and for most curlers, it probably was. However, Colleen Jones was playing her favourite shot, the out-turn hit, and the rest is history. My advice to you is not to worry about calling the right or wrong shot. My dad always used to say, "If you call the wrong shot, and you make it, it was the right shot!"

Your team will find out soon enough what its strong points are, and the trick will be to dictate the style of play before your opponent does. If you are able to bring the game to your opponent and force them to play on your terms, more often than not, you'll find yourself in the winner's circle.

PLAYING TO YOUR OPPONENT'S WEAKNESSES

In hockey, if your team is playing against an opponent with small wingers who don't like to mix it up along the boards or in the corners, it might be wise to play a physical game where you generate scoring chances by outmuscling the other team. In curling, the same mentality might apply.

The trick is to discover a team's weakness, and discover it quickly. The earliest opportunity to analyze your next opponent would be to scout them visually in a prior game or in the 10-minute practice session that each team has. It never ceases to amaze me how many teams at a provincial, national, or international competition throw their 10 minutes of practice rocks and then walk off the ice to wait for the game to start; they miss out on the opportunity to watch the releases of the four competitors they are about to play. In a 10-minute practice, your opponent can throw all eight rocks six to eight times, representing six to eight ends' worth of valuable feedback.

What an advantage it is to know their weaknesses before the game even begins. If I find a member of the opposition who has an inside-out release (which causes the rock to drift, for example, on the out-turn), I will take every chance I get to draw around a guard on the out-turn side, thus exploiting my competition's weakness. If nothing else, you start your game with a mental edge when you think you have found an advantage! Watching opponents practise also provides you with additional time to read the ice and the way the rocks are behaving.

AGGRESSIVE STYLE

There are some players and teams who are notoriously aggressive. They want to pour rocks into the house and dare you to mix it up with them. They have a firm belief in their ability to score five or six if given the opportunity, and are confident that they can minimize your scoring if they get into trouble.

Perhaps two of the most famous players who fit this description are the Alberta duo of Kevin Martin and Randy Ferbey. Both of these superstars are more than willing to get into a slugging match with you and pull out a 9–7 or 9–8 game. In Randy's case, he has such a clutch fourth in David Nedohin that, no matter what shot he needs to win or escape an end, he knows that David will make the draw to the button to save the end 99 times out of 100. Kevin, meanwhile, is so accurate with heavy weight that he can afford to play this way, knowing that the opposition rarely has him in any sort of trouble.

An aggressive strategy is most often used when you are down on the scoreboard. The free guard zone is your friend if your team uses it to your advantage. For example, say you are two down with the hammer, playing the sixth end. The team with the two-point lead will put its rock on the button. You counter by throwing the corner guard. Note: the location of the guard depends on your opponent and ice conditions. If I'm playing Kevin Martin, I might want the corner guard longer, in the 1 position, because, later in the end, Kevin will be looking for runbacks, and the longer the guards are, the tougher his shot will be. If I'm playing Randy Ferbey, I'll probably throw the guard a little tighter to the rings, in the 3 position, where it is more advantageous for our team to tap back later in the end. The opposition will probably play on top of the rock they have already thrown into the rings.

If you are trying to score multiple points, avoid the urge to play the easy double. Even if you make the double and your shooter rolls out, your opponent would now have the opportunity to peel off the lone corner guard, and your scoring chance for this end, in theory, is gone. Throw the second corner guard on the other side of the sheet. Now the game is on: you have two corner guards in place.

DEFENSIVE STYLE

When I talk about defensive play, I am not talking about it in negative terms. A defensive strategy in the game of curling is as effective as an aggressive style. It involves keeping the house as clean as possible and working towards winning the end or the game with last shot. Used correctly, it is a strategy that will most certainly keep you in games and allow you to hang around long enough to win.

With the four-rock rule, defending a lead has become much more complex. Obviously, your main goal is to remove all enemy rocks—and, for that matter, all of your own. The four-rock rule allows the opposition two free chances at placing guards. I can't stress enough that the more accurately you can throw the peel weight, the better your chance of recovering from this deficit. Your objective is to clear the front and roll the shooter out of the playing surface. Many teams make the mistake of guarding the shot rock that has been ignored by the team that needs the points. Simply put, when you are leading in the game, every rock in play is detrimental.

BALANCED STYLE

A balanced style of play simply means that you combine an aggressive style with a

Many teams make the mistake of guarding the shot rock that has been ignored by the team that needs the points.

defensive style and adjust as the situation demands. Even the most ardent proponents of aggressive and defensive styles of play use a balanced approach at some point.

You need to be willing and able to used a balanced approach at various times, or you leave yourself and your rink vulnerable. If you cannot convert from either mode of play to something a little more balanced, teams will ultimately figure it out and take advantage of it.

Let me cite an example from Torino as an illustration of how we used a balanced game plan to perfection.

In the winner-take-all semifinal against Pete Fenson of the USA, we decided that we would come out very aggressively and force Pete to make difficult shot after difficult shot. The strategy worked better than we could have imagined, as we were answering his single scores with deuces. By the sixth end, we were up 6–3 and in a position to basically shut it down and force him to create much tougher scoring opportunities. With the quality of hitters that I felt we had

on our team, it made perfect sense to switch from offence to defence in the hopes of forcing Team USA to take more and more chances, especially without the aid of last rock, as the game wore on. Finally, in the ninth end, even though we were only one up with the hammer, Fenson was committed to gamble, knowing that a multiple score for us would end the game.

As a by-product of our patience in the last few ends, we were presented with a chance to salt it away with a five-ender in the ninth and, for all intents and purposes, it was over.

PERSPECTIVE

Even if you're vying for Olympic gold, you can always find time to learn a lesson in perspective. A pledge to lighten up and enjoy the moment became a defining moment for Team Gushue in Torino.

We began our week playing very well. Hard-fought victories against Germany's Andy Kapp and Norway's Pal Trulsen had placed us in a very comfortable position at four wins and a loss. Then the wheels began to fall off. Consecutive defeats to Finland and host Italy put us on the brink of being shut out of the playoffs. It was time to put our heads together and find a way to turn the ship around.

During our daily players' meeting after the loss to Italy, we began to dissect our game and our approach to the competition, and we came to the conclusion that we weren't having any fun, that we had failed to keep things in perspective. Here we were in the middle of the most amazing experience of our lives, and we weren't allowing ourselves to enjoy a single second of it. Frankly, we needed to lighten up.

It is no coincidence that our game took off after that meeting. We stopped pressing and overreacting to every error and simply allowed our natural talent and experience to take over. Once we got things back into focus, we were virtually unstoppable.

You might find yourself in the same situation. Everyone wants to play, and everyone wants to win. Sometimes, you just have to let the game come to you. Remember, it is just a game. If you can remind yourself of that every once in a while, you'll find yourself enjoying the sport much more—and playing much better as well.

THE PERILS OF OVERPREPARATION

It is easy to buy into the mindset that spending countless hours scouting the opposition or practising a certain technique over and over again are necessary in order to get better. But if you're breathing, eating, and sleeping the game of curling, then you are probably trying too hard.

I think the Randy Ferbey rink might have fallen into that trap just before the 2005 Olympic trials. Their schedule might have left them winded as they began the tournament.

For those of us who can't get enough of curling, there is always going to be that temptation to do more. But like anything else, moderation is the key, and you need to be aware of the pitfalls of overpreparation.

HAVE FUN

If you're having fun, you'll play better. It isn't a coincidence that my most enjoyable years in the sport were 1987, 1993, and 2006—years in which I won World and Olympic championships. Watch world-class curlers like Norway's Pal Trulsen and Dordi Nordby play, and you can see that they are smiling, joking around, and chatting with team members and the opposition. They're having fun and enjoying the game.

5

CHESS ON ICE

SHOT SELECTION AND STRATEGY

"If you call the wrong shot and you make it, it was the right shot."
—**BILL HOWARD** (my dad)

IN THE 1980S, Al Hackner, a skip from northern Ontario, was notorious for his ability to remain cool under pressure. No matter what twists or turns a particular game took, Al always seemed prepared. It was no accident: Hackner, aptly nicknamed "The Iceman," was always one or two shots ahead of the opposition skip, and because of this anticipation he was ready to deal with opportunity or crisis with equal aplomb.

Curling is often compared to chess: you have to be thinking one or more shots ahead and be very aware of what your opponent may decide to do. You have to be thinking, "If I do this, they will do that, and that will mean that I can—or will have to—do this." Playing each shot as a distinct problem on its own will not allow you to control the "run of play" and keep the game in your control.

The art of strategy and shot selection also lies in knowing that your teammates can execute the requested shots. It only makes sense, but it's easy to overlook.

SHOTS

A curler has numerous shots in his arsenal; these are the common ones.

DRAW (ALSO GUARD)

There are basically only two types of draw shots: a rock that is drawn successfully into the rings, and a rock that is drawn successfully into the free guard zone, which would be categorized as a guard. The draw into the rings is for the purpose of scoring points; the purpose of the guard would be to set up the end.

HIT

A hit is simply a rock thrown with enough force to remove your opponent's rock (or in some cases, your own rock) from play. There are various hitting weights:

Hack weight. A slow-moving shot that barely removes the target rock.

Normal weight. The weight the thrower would ordinarily throw on a consistent basis (and ideally, the entire team would throw the same weight on a consistent basis) and is hard enough, when placed with certainty, to remove the target rock.

Up weight or peel weight. A shot delivered at a very high speed to remove or promote the target rock.

When you are attempting to hit a rock, you must be conscious of both the curl in the ice and the speed at which you are throwing the rock. Curling is no different than golf, where, if you have a six-foot putt on a green that has a noticeable slope from right to left, you may be able to allow two, four, or even six inches of break, and still be successful at holing the putt as long as you have chosen to hit the golf ball at the appropriate speed. Obviously, the harder you hit the golf ball, the less time there will be for the ball to break. If a hack-weight takeout is thrown on relatively swingy ice, because it takes 20 seconds for the rock to reach its goal, it will curl roughly twice as much as a peel- or up-weight shot that would take only 10 seconds to travel the same distance.

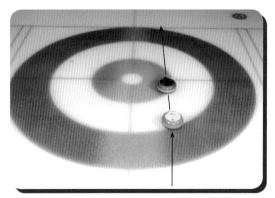

The takeout shot is simply a rock thrown with enough force to remove another from play. But it's not always as simple as firing the rock down the ice.

TYPES OF GUARDS

BECAUSE ANY ROCK THROWN into the free guard zone may not be removed by an opponent until the fifth rock of the end, it's important to use your early shots to set up guards.

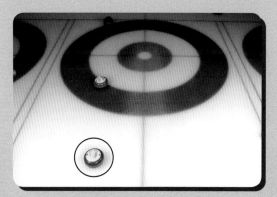

The corner guard (circled) is a draw shot placed some distance ahead of the house, to one side of the centre line. A team with the hammer (last rock) will almost always use their first shot to set a corner guard, because it increases their chances of scoring multiple points.

A long guard is a guard placed well short of the house. Long guards are useful if your team plays a finesse game. If you don't have the hammer, setting a centre guard, as shown here, can give you control over the middle and prevent your opponent from scoring extra points.

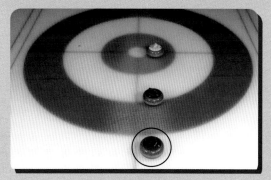

By contrast, the short (also known as tight) guard is delivered so that it stops close to the rings. If your team plays a strong hitting game, you'll benefit by setting these up in front of your opponent's counters, allowing you to play the short, easier raise.

RAISE

A raise is a rock that is promoted forward. The raised rock can be promoted behind a guard, into scoring position, or into a position to set up a future shot.

FREEZE

The freeze is one of the more difficult shots in curling, demanding precision, weight control, and alignment. The perfect freeze is created when your rock comes to rest touching your opponent's rock and lined up directly in front of it. Under most ice conditions, a successful freeze is very difficult to remove because of the proximity of the back rock. A freeze that has the appropriate weight and is virtually touching your opponent's rock, but is off-centre, is called a corner freeze, and can be more easily removed,

but it will be deflected at a pre-determined angle. The corner freeze can be used to your advantage in certain situations.

TICK

A tick is a shot invented in direct response to the free guard zone rule. Within the free guard zone, the first two opponent's rocks may be moved, but not removed from play. To move an opponent's rock off to the side without removing it from play, I would recommend a very lightweight takeout between hack weight and back-line weight—in some cases, T-line weight. The objective here is to control the scoring zone in front of the rings, inside the four-foot slide path. If the shot is executed properly, the opponent's rock will be promoted off to one side of the sheet, and your shooter will

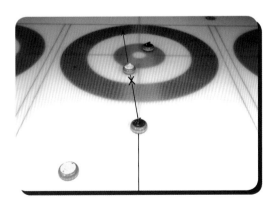

A rock can be promoted forward and knock a third rock out of play. Here, Blue raises its own rock, sending Yellow out of the rings.

Blue executes a perfect freeze. Their rock has stopped right in front of the yellow rock, making it very difficult for Yellow to remove without also taking out their own rock.

roll to the other side of the sheet or out of play, achieving the goal of keeping the front open for your skip's last shot.

STRATEGY

Beginning curlers are unlikely to skip much, except in funspiels or special events, but it helps to know approximately where strategies come from.

While there are numerous considerations that go into how you approach the game, here are the fundamentals:

- Do you have the last shot (the "hammer")?
- What are the skill levels of your teammates? Who can draw?
- Who can hit?
- How accurate is each player?
- What is your skill level when it comes to hits and draws, and which is most comfortable for you?

If you have the hammer, it is a good idea to play the sides of the house and keep the approach to the four-foot circle open if possible. This way you can try to save a situation with a draw, or, if you have one or more rocks in scoring position, add a point with the final draw. If you eventually want to skip, you should develop your draw weight.

If you do not have the hammer, do

TYPES OF HITS

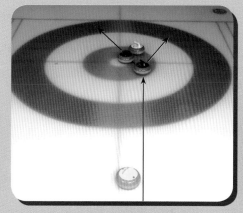

The double takeout.

HIT AND STAY: a hit that removes the opponent's rock, replacing it with your own.

HIT AND ROLL: a hit that removes the opponent's rock, after which your shooter continues to move (or "rolls") to a desired location.

DOUBLE OR TRIPLE TAKEOUTS: hits that remove two or three of your opponent's rocks.

HIT AND ROLL OUT: a hit that removes the opponent's rock, after which your own rock rolls out of the rings (commonly used to blank an end and retain last shot).

PEEL: a variation of the hit and roll in which the stationary rock is struck off-centre, causing it to roll out of play on one side while the shooter goes out of play on the other side.

the exact opposite. Play the middle and the front, block the four-foot circle, and try to bump one of your rocks in—or make bumping one of your rocks in a really risky proposition for your opponent.

FREE GUARD ZONE

For decades, the sport was dominated by a game-day strategy centred around getting an early lead and peeling your opponent's rocks until they simply ran out of them. It was a strategy that kept traditionalists happy, but did little to enhance the excitement of the game and attract new curlers.

Beginning in 1984, in an effort to become better shot makers, my brother Glenn and I began to experiment with the idea that the first four rocks of an end could not be removed from play, no matter where they were. In our one-on-one scrimmages featuring this innovation, we were forced to deal with many more rocks in play, which in turn demanded that we play shots with a higher degree of difficulty. Ultimately, what became the "four-rock free guard zone rule" improved our skills with finesse shots and gave us a number of strategic weapons that other teams lacked. For nearly five years, the idea was our little secret, until a twist of fate brought it into the public domain for the very first time.

Moncton, New Brunswick, a city I now call home, celebrated its 100th anniversary in 1990. As part of the celebrations, the biggest bonspiel in the history of curling, the Moncton 100, was organized. The top 16 teams in the world were invited to compete for a top prize of $250,000. In an attempt to bring a fresh feel to the game, Doug Maxwell, one of the bonspiel's co-ordinators, asked me for advice on how to spice up the event. I told Doug about the drill Glenn and I had devised. He loved the idea and ran with it for the bonspiel, and, for all intents and purposes, the "Moncton Rule" was born.

After some hesitation from other participating teams, the rule was incorporated, and its impact was obvious and immediate. Curling had become mundane and predictable with the emphasis on defence; in most cases, a one- or two-point lead was insurmountable. With the combination of more consistent ice conditions and better deliveries, the defensive takeout game, although skillful, was killing the sport.

This fact was obvious at the 1989 Brier, where Pat Ryan defeated Rick Folk. To the trained eye, it was a well curled, defensive final. But as the game progressed, the capacity crowd began to chant "Boring!" The average curling fan watching at home couldn't have been blamed for reaching for the remote.

The Moncton Rule is simple: the first four rocks of an end cannot be removed. This creates tremendous offensive chances, eliminating the defensive strategy forever. I am a strong believer that offence sells. With multiple rocks in play in virtually every end, the game has been opened up, raising the importance—and level—of strategy and shot making. The spectators loved the changes, and the 16 teams that attended the Moncton 100 in 1989 were so impressed that the idea was taken back to the European associations, who immediately adopted it into their official rules of play.

The free guard zone is defined as the area from the far hog line to the tee line, excluding the house. The original concept was that none of the opponent's rocks within this area could be moved to a place where they would need to be removed from play until after the fourth rock had been delivered (the "three-rock rule"). The international community went a step further: they ruled that none of the opposing team's rocks in this area could be removed from play until the fifth rock had been delivered (the "four-rock rule"). Canada has since adopted this interpretation.

The free guard zone can (and should) be

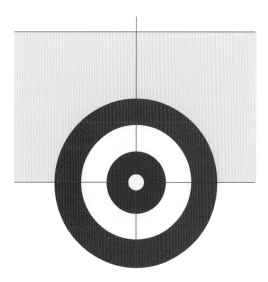

The free guard zone (shown in yellow) is the area between the hog line and the tee line excluding the house.

used to put up guards for later use. Use it this way, and you'll have the advantage. If you draw into the house with any of the first rocks, they can be hit and removed from play. If you play them out in front, they can be moved, but not taken out of play immediately. You may, however, move your opponent's rocks into the house so that they may be removed on a subsequent shot. And remember that the rule applies only to your opponent's rocks: removing any of your own rocks is permitted.

When you have the hammer, consider setting up corner guards at the sides of the centre line and drawing around these to get a rock into scoring position while leaving

STYLES OF PLAY

KEEPING IT CLEAN

If you are confident and accurate with hits, you can force your opponent to play a hitting game, too, thus requiring them to play to your strength. The key is to use hits where your rock stays in the house. If you have the hammer, you can play with an eye towards scoring with the last rock by hitting a rock and staying to score, or towards taking all rocks out of the house, allowing you to keep the hammer to try for a multiple score in the next end. If you do not have the hammer, hitting is one way to ensure that your opponent will not get more than one point and that they will need to make a draw to do so—or, at least, play a hit with the risk of rolling out.

JUNKING IT UP

If your forte is the draw and the finesse shot, you can play the odds by placing guards and building a bit of a wall across the house to hide behind. If you are playing a hitting team, keep replacing the guards on the principle that even the best shooters miss, or partially miss, and you will get a chance to draw in to cover. Another finesse play is to clutter up the front and bump one of your rocks into scoring position with what is, essentially, a slightly heavy draw.

the centre four-foot area open for a draw. Without the hammer, set up short and/or long centre guards that you can draw around to a scoring position while making the opposition's draw options less attractive by denying them the four-foot circle.

GENERAL STRATEGIES WITHOUT LAST ROCK
DEFENCE

In situations where the score is close or a team is ahead in points, "defensive" is the word that will best describe the approach of a team that doesn't have last rock. In these situations, skips will attempt to apply a strategy that limits the opposition to scoring only one point. To accomplish this, knowledgeable skips will direct play towards the centre of the sheet, thus restricting the opposition's ability to spread their rocks out. This may ultimately block the opposition's path to the four-foot circle, thus enhancing the opportunity to steal one or more points. Teams without last rock are usually more cautious in their shot selection, in that takeouts are favoured over draw shots when opponents have rocks in the rings.

Teams without last rock, who, as a result of the situation (score, end, ice, or opposition), would prefer to play a defensive style of game are faced with an interesting dilemma. Their lead cannot remove any opposition rock from the free guard zone, and, as a result, they have few shot-selection options available. The final decision will be greatly dependent upon the skill level of the lead. Remember: in many situations, giving up a deuce will be perfectly acceptable.

OFFENCE

Thanks to the free guard zone rule, orchestrating offence without last rock is very easy. The placement of centre guards that cannot be removed by the opposition until the fifth rock of the end can produce a number of opportunities for a team to control centre ice and potentially steal one or more points. The only major concern for the skip without last rock is whether the skip with the hammer will elect to come around the centre guard. The farther out the centre guard is, the more likely the last-rock skip will be to play an aggressive come-around draw in search of multiple points.

GENERAL STRATEGIES WITH LAST ROCK
OFFENCE

In situations where early ends have passed and the score is close or a team is down in

points, a focus on offence is the best approach for teams with last-rock advantage. Knowledgeable skips may direct play to the sides of the sheet, enabling them to

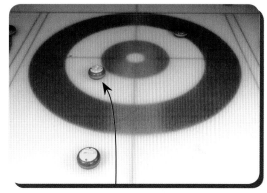

Last-rock skips will often use a come-around draw to pick up an extra point.

spread their rocks out. This also tends to keep the path to the four-foot circle open for a possible end-saving last-rock draw shot.

Last-rock teams will attempt to initiate their offence to the side of the sheet by establishing a corner guard, but they may also find themselves developing offensive opportunities on centre ice in an attempt to prevent a potential steal. Aggressive last-rock skips will take advantage of centre guards by playing come-around draws in an effort to score multiple points, even though this strategy will increase the risk of a steal. Ice conditions may also force last-rock skips

CONTROL THE FRONT

The area just short of the rings is where the battle is won or lost. Most novice teams ignore opponent's rocks that are short of the rings, and it inevitably comes back to haunt them. Fight the urge to hold shot rock early in the end. Keeping in mind the golden rule, "control the front," will give you the most options as the end progresses. Remember, if your second's rock comes up a little short, you have four more shots to make it better.

to direct play towards the centre of the sheet if rocks are not curling much from the centre line out.

It is important to note that it is common practice for a skip who cannot score more than a single point in the end to throw the final rock through the house or to hit and roll out, thus blanking the end and keeping last-rock advantage.

DEFENCE

Teams with last-rock advantage who would prefer a defensive style of play because of the score, ice conditions, or the relative abilities of the opposing teams, have a number of shot-selection options available to them. Their objective may well be to ensure the opposition does not have the opportunity to steal points; therefore, controlling centre ice will be a key factor. If the opposition lead places a centre guard, the last-rock skip will have to decide which of several defensive options best suits the situation.

READING THE ICE

The importance of reading ice cannot be overemphasized. It often represents the difference between making and missing shots, and it is what separates the great skips from the rest of the pack. Over the course of a 10-end game, your team will throw 80 rocks, which means that a skip will see 160 rocks, plus those thrown in both team practices. As the game progresses, the ice conditions will change—the pebble will become worn down—affecting the path those rocks follow. The key is to concentrate for the entire game.

Using the tee line as your guide for broom positioning, it is very easy to use the different-coloured circles that intersect the tee line to observe the amount of curl the rock takes from each location. If a rock curls three feet on average, for example, and you need four feet of ice to draw from the outside to the centre line,

Reading the ice is every player's responsibility.

logic tells you that from the centre line to the outside, the rock will curve only two feet. Visualize the shots and create a mental map of the different areas of the sheet—I find the easiest way to do this is to picture a cross-section of the sheet. In the above example, this sheet would be in the shape of a bowl, with the bottom of the bowl being on the centre line; thus, rocks curling outside-in curl more than rocks trying to go uphill when shooting inside-out.

Reading the ice is every player's responsibility. Players should make an effort to familiarize themselves with the curl of turns, both from the centre of the sheet to the outside and from the outside towards centre. Learn the ice for draws and take-outs, commit this knowledge to memory, and update it as the game progresses.

Improving your ice-reading skills comes only through practice and hard work. Again, curling isn't much different from golf in this respect. One key factor in Tiger Woods's success is his ability to read the putts. (If I were to read the putts for Tiger Woods, he wouldn't win a nickel.) Reading the putts and reading the ice are acquired skills.

THE HUMAN FACTOR

One of the key ingredients to being a good skip is understanding and maximizing the abilities of your team while trying to take advantage of any opposition weaknesses.

Consider Jamie Korab, the lead for the 2006 Olympic team. Jamie has a slight drift from right to left in his curling delivery, and a wonderful soft release on his out-turn. This means that his out-turns curl like crazy while his in-turns run relatively straight. To the inexperienced skip, this would be a negative. To me, it became an advantage, and we affectionately called Jamie's out-turn "the weapon." By recognizing the tremendous curl to his out-turn and putting the broom in the right spot, we accomplished two things: we were able to bury rocks quite easily on straight ice with his out-turn, and we managed to exploit an opposition weakness because they simply could not follow Jamie's out-turn.

All aspiring curlers are taught to throw

the rock "perfectly." Although we all want to achieve the perfect curling delivery, that doesn't necessarily mean we all have to fit into the same mould. Consider that Tiger Woods and Jim Furyk have entirely different techniques, yet they are two of the best golfers in the world. Skips and coaches must acknowledge that their players will have idiosyncrasies and make appropriate adjustments and allowances. For example, the majority of curlers I have played with, when asked to throw hack weight, will overthrow this shot later in the game. The skip who knows this will adjust the ice accordingly.

When it comes to developing a team game plan and making shot-selection decisions, I strongly recommend that you factor in the strengths of your individual players—know each player's best shot, preferred weight, most consistent turn, and even weight-judging skills and sweeping ability.

Confidence comes with success and is the key factor in developing a winning attitude. Whenever possible, allow your players to play the shots they have the greatest chance of making. This was never so evident than when I joined the boys from The Rock to compete in two spiels before the Olympic trials.

The very first end I skipped was against Pal Trulsen from Norway. I played my usual aggressive, "pull-the-goalie" style in the first end, but after a couple of shots were missed the wrong way, and the Norwegians demonstrated great shotmaking, my style left Brad Gushue (who was throwing the last two rocks) two difficult finesse shots that were unsuccessful—Trulsen scored four.

I immediately realized that we had to play slightly more cautiously for the first few ends, until the youngsters familiarized themselves with the ice and rocks. As I became more familiar with the team, I realized the team's real strength was its ability to play the runbacks and multiple hits with our back end. Our strategy then evolved so that the first two throwers became very aggressive, often freezing to our opponent's rocks while leaving them shot, controlling the front, and allowing the back end to run the rocks in to create multiple scores. We realized that at the world level, our front end had an advantage over most other teams at playing the aggressive game, and our game plan was adjusted to play these teams.

THE OPPOSITION

As in other sports, knowledge of your opponent is essential to the development of a winning game plan. Knowing the players' individual strengths and weaknesses in all components of the game will help you develop your strategy, and so will an analysis of their strategic approach to the game in a variety of situations.

Scouting the opposition prior to a big game is well worth the time and should provide you with the opportunity to enter the game completely prepared. In the Olympic final, we faced Finland, who had the hottest skip in the competition. We analyzed all the available data and found the Finnish front end had been weaker on in-turns that particular week, and they played a very defensive style with a tendency to lean towards their bread-and-butter shot, the high hard one, which the skip and vice were very good at. We also knew this firsthand because they had defeated us in the round robin with this strategy.

So we decided to be very aggressive with our front end, which was our strength. Jamie and I played a lot of come-arounds and finesse shots, which we knew from the past was probably the weakest part of Finland's game.

The payoff came in the sixth end. Even though we had only a one-point lead with the hammer, the Finnish team decided to play aggressively themselves, and at the last part of that end, the vice and skip were

BEATING THE CLOCK

If you are one of those teams that has trouble with the time clocks, look beyond your strategy decisions in your effort to save time. Quite often, there will be one or two players per team who waste valuable seconds looking for their rocks when they should already be in the hack, with their rocks cleaned off, ready for their skip's call. Ten seconds doesn't sound like much time, but if you multiply it by 80 rocks, your team will have wasted more than 13 minutes!

forced to make three very difficult come-around shots. We had successfully forced them towards a weaker part of their game.

SHOT CLOCK

In the past, there was no time limit for skips and teams to arrive at a shot decision in tournaments. Every club had its criminally slow players, and as tournament prizes became more lucrative, the increased importance of each shot caused this disease to creep into tournament play.

As television coverage of curling grew, the variable length of games was a potential nightmare. Broadcasters needed to meet their schedules, so it was critical that games take place within a particular, and relatively predictable, time frame. The result was the introduction of a time clock; teams were limited to 73 minutes each in which to complete a 10-end game, with a mandatory five-minute break after five ends.

According to the rules, when a team's time clock runs out, the opposing team will win if they are ahead at the time, or if they are trailing they may try to win by continuing to play until their clock runs out. Suddenly, it was a wise strategy to play the opening ends quickly and build up a "cushion" of time for critical late-game decisions. I can vividly remember one team from Quebec that had the habit of holding long conversations before and after almost every shot. Their poor management of the shot clock early in games came back to haunt them on more than one occasion, as they were forced to hurry their shots in the ninth and tenth ends. By using up so much of their allotted time early in the contest, they forfeited the opportunity to strategize before game-breaking shots late in the fray.

On the other hand, playing opening ends too quickly can also backfire. In an event I played in Scotland in 1987—before anyone in Canada had used time clocks—we were so worried about running out of time that we ran around as fast as we could. At the fifth-end break we had 48 minutes left, having used only 32. This was comforting, but we were now down 5–1 because we hadn't taken the appropriate time to think about what we were doing.

Most competitive games allow you more than seven minutes an end, which is nearly one minute per shot—ample time to complete the game. Practise playing an end in five minutes so that you have the confidence to do it if you have to.

PUTTING STRATEGY INTO ACTION

20 SCENARIOS

Remember that it's not the shot you make, it's the shot you leave for your opponent that counts!

WHEN YOU'VE CURLED as long as I have, you see patterns and situations that occur regularly. And, of course, after a game you replay it in your mind, reviewing different shot options and perhaps wondering what you might have done differently. Every curler is different, and shot selection ultimately depends on the skill of your teammates, but here is some advice for 20 common scenarios. Keep in mind that when it comes to making the right call, you also have to think of the smart way to miss the shot, and most importantly, remember that it's not the shot you make, it's the shot you leave for your opponent that counts!

SCENARIO 1: THE PERFECT MISS

With the score tied, Blue has thrown a centre guard with a free guard zone rock **(1)**. This is a very common situation at the start of an end. The obvious answer would be for the yellow team to counter by drawing around the guard, but to where? Too close to the button, and the blue team can freeze in front of your rock, making it tough to score two or more points.

The perfect miss would be just short of the rings **(2a)**. This rock cannot be removed by the blue team until the fifth rock has been thrown, and maybe, later in the end, Yellow can tap it into a better position behind cover.

Another approach would be to play the come-around narrow, either burying the rock or, if you wreck, moving the centre blue guard over to the side of the sheet and rolling to the other side **(2b)**, leaving the front scoring area open and hopefully dictating play to the sides of the sheet.

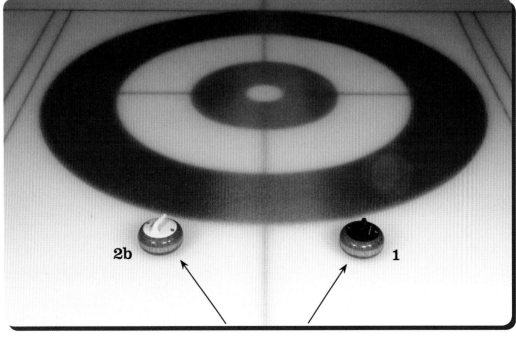

SCENARIO 2: WATCH YOUR TESTOSTERONE

Here is a scenario that very few teams figure out. With the score tied and Yellow with the hammer, Blue draws to the top four-foot **(1)**, Yellow counters with a corner guard **(2)**, and Blue plays **(3)** into the rings, setting up the easy double.

In this case, if you're on the yellow team, I can't advise strongly enough that you throw hack weight only—resist the urge to fire big weight at the blue rocks. The harder you throw your hit, the tougher it is for your rock to stay in play. If you roll out attempting the double, the blue team, if they are smart, will peel the guard **(2)**, taking away the opportunity to score more than one. The good miss here is to miss the double by throwing light **(4)**, while still moving the blue rocks behind the tee line, where they may be used later.

Making the double looks good but doesn't score any points.

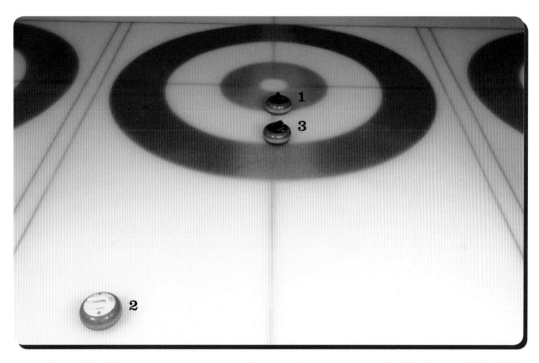

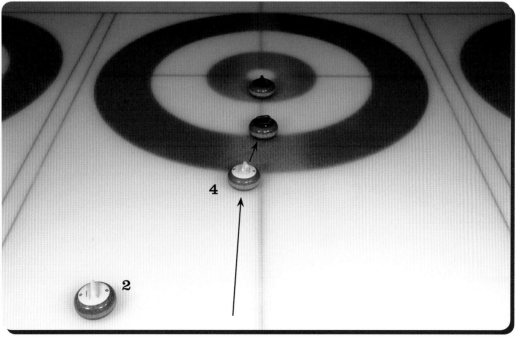

SCENARIO 3: WHY DID THEY DO THAT?

You are Blue, with a rock on the edge of the four-foot **(3)**. Yellow has one rock off to the side in the rings **(4)** and a corner guard a little to the left **(5)**. Your team is ahead by a few points, and it's early in the end. Resist hitting the rock in the rings—remember that your opponent put up the corner guard for a reason! If you go after the shot in the rings, Yellow will draw around the guard under cover, setting up a multiple score. Instead, peel the corner guard towards the other yellow, rolling your shooter out of play. If you're successful, you eliminate the chance for your opponent to score more than one. If you remove the guard, the most you should give up is two, with many opportunities to make a double or for your opponent to roll out.

You don't have to hit the rock in the rings.

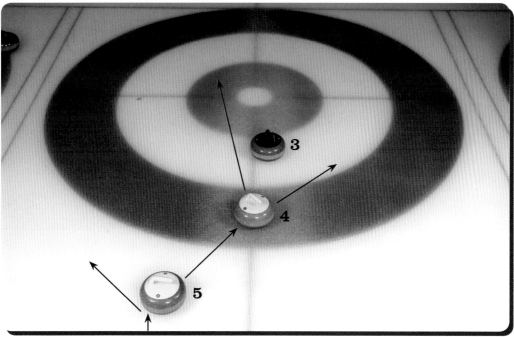

SCENARIO 4: DON'T ALWAYS GO BY THE BOOK

Sometimes you can't see the forest for the trees! With a two-point lead in the last end of our final game of the Olympic trials in Halifax, we threw first (Blue) and missed the wrong way, ending up with a centre guard **(1)** that could only help Jeff Stoughton, our opponent. If I had a dime for every time a fan has asked me why Jeff didn't throw a corner guard for their next shot, I could probably retire. Nearly every coach would call for the corner guard, exposing our mistake, which we could then remove. Under the free guard zone rules, if Jeff's team had elected to throw the corner guard, we would have peeled our own guard, leaving one less chance for a two- or three-point end. Stoughton, veteran that he is, called for their rock to be drawn into a position **(2)** that prevented our team from eliminating our own rock.

The rules are there to help you.

SCENARIO 5: MORE IS BETTER

It's late in the game and your team (Yellow) is down three or four points. Here's a standard scenario: Blue has rocks at the top of the four-foot **(1)** and at the top of the 12-foot **(3)**. You've set a corner guard **(2)**. Blue, in all likelihood, will hit everything in sight, so counter by separating your rocks **(4)** to prevent a double. Fight the urge to hit the opposition rocks in the rings. At this point, the more rocks in play, the better!

SCENARIO 6: UNCONVENTIONAL WISDOM

It's the beginning of an end, the score is close, and you have last rock. Better still, your opponent has missed a wide-open takeout, leaving your yellow rock over to the left-hand side of the sheet.

Conventional wisdom suggests splitting the rings. That would not be the wrong call, but let's think about it: to score your two, you'd have to execute seven perfect shots, all the while hoping that your opponent doesn't make one double!

Instead, try guarding the rock in the rings **(2)**. If your opponent tries to hit the back rock and misses the wrong way (which is wide), you now have the potential for three. In addition, if the opposition removes your back rock, you always have the corner guard to use for cover, to generate a multiple score.

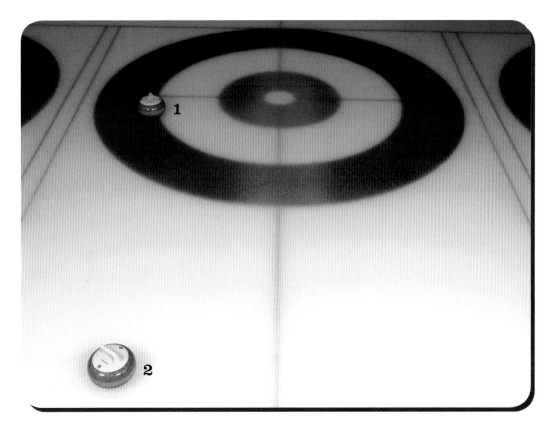

SCENARIO 7: UNDER COVER

It's the last end, and you (Yellow) need three points to tie. You have a corner guard **(2)**, but the opposition has two staggered rocks **(1, 3)** in the rings.

Do not hit the enemy rocks! In this scenario, the blue rocks are your allies.

With the blue rocks angled, your play should be to draw around the blue rocks **(4)**. Even if your rock is not shot rock, it is in the scoring area. If Blue remove just one of their own rocks at the top of the rings, you can now go around the corner guard and have two rocks buried behind cover. If your opponent is unsuccessful in removing either buried rock, you can tap out the **1** rock and stay for three points.

Sometimes the other skip, because he has shot rock, decides not to hit—you have a much better chance of a multiple score.

Your opponent's rocks can be your friends.

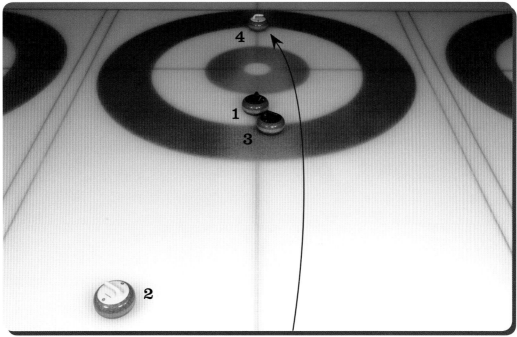

SCENARIO 8: THINK FIRST

This time, you don't have last rock, so you have thrown up a centre guard **(1)**. Yellow has countered with a corner guard **(2)**. You set up the centre guard for a reason, so draw around it! But remember, Yellow has countered with a corner guard for a reason, too. Most ice surfaces don't allow you to completely bury your rock behind the centre guard. With that in mind, draw around the centre with the out-turn **(3)** exposing the right half of your rock, forcing your opponent to the right and leaving you a simple wide-open takeout shot. If you draw around to the left side of the centre guard, your opponent may hit and roll to the left side of the sheet behind the corner guard, leaving you a much tougher shot.

Make your next shot easier.

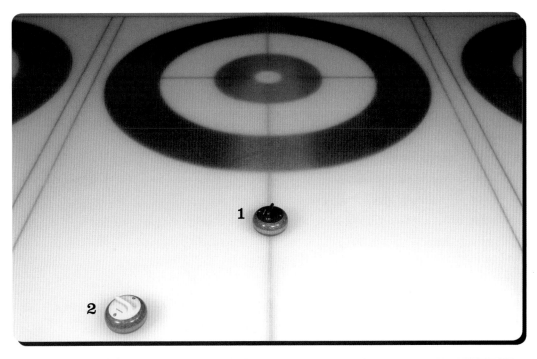

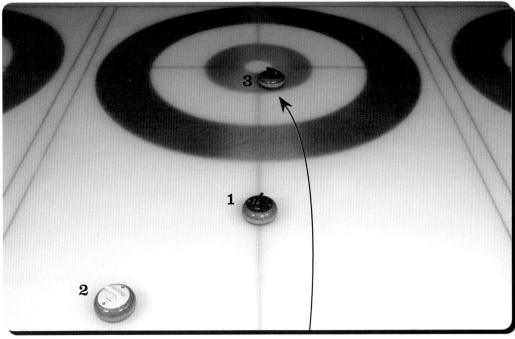

SCENARIO 9: TRICK SHOT

Here, two blue rocks **(1, 2)** are lined up with the yellow rock in the rings **(3)** and are touching, or frozen to, each other. If you've played billiards at all, you already know that striking any part of the front ball will send the second ball directly towards ball number three. However, because curling rocks have rough striking bands, rock **2** will try to react on the same angle that rock **1** was hit on by rock **4**. I encourage you and your team to experiment with these angles. We had this exact situation at the Moncton 100 against Eddie Werenich. Luckily, it was his shot that came off on a very weird angle, allowing us to win the game and, more importantly, learn the angles. If rock **4** hits rock **1** thin enough, rock **2** will completely miss yellow rock **3**.

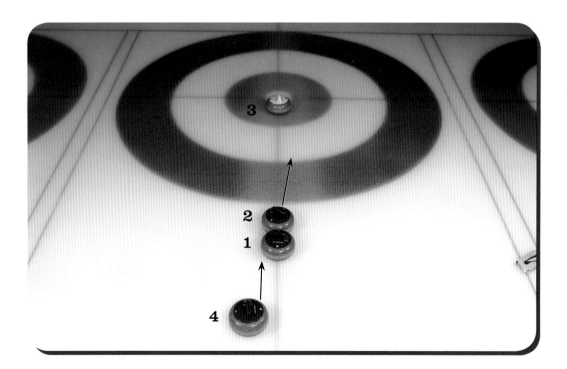

SCENARIO 10: MORE THAN ONE WAY TO SKIN A CAT

Your opponent (Yellow) has their rock **(2)** buried on the out-turn side, just behind the tee line, early in the end. There is more than one option, but I think there is only one correct miss. (Hitting the yellow rock **(2)** and rolling to where you are buried would be very difficult.)

Since the yellow rock is behind the tee line, the best call would be the freeze. In this situation, most teams use the out-turn to attempt the freeze, since the object rock is open on that side, but this strategy will make it easier to remove. I like to use the in-turn for two reasons: first, if I am successful, my rock **(3)** will be buried; second, I have the luxury of being able to be light.

A second option: using the natural angle, rock **4** will be very difficult to remove without jamming on Yellow's rock **(2)**. Plus, if your opponent elects to guard your raise, you then have the out-turn tap to lie two. I now have options on both sides.

SCENARIO 11: A GOOD OFFENCE IS A GREAT DEFENCE

The score is tied in the last end, you have the hammer, and your opponent, Blue, throws a centre guard **(1)**.

Decision time: do you attempt the tick, risking the complete miss, or do you ignore the dangerous centre guard and draw around it **(2)**? This situation can be debated until the bartender goes home! The advantage that you have as the skip of the yellow team is that you know what the other team is going to do.

I like to play the draw to position **(2)**; the blue team will invariably throw the second centre guard **(3)**. I will counter with another buried rock **(4)** in the top half of the rings. This accomplishes two things: first, Blue is going to have a tough time getting shot rock, and if they do, my team has a very easy raise to win; second, Yellow can now attempt a double peel on the dangerous front rocks without having to worry about rocks on the sides of the sheet that might cause problems.

Another variation would be to try the tick shot on your first attempt and, if it works, do it again on your second shot. If it doesn't work the first time, Yellow is faced with two centre guards, so you switch strategy, throwing a draw with your second shot to position **(2)**, thereby controlling the four-foot.

Keep the pressure on your opponent.

SCENARIO 12: THE STING

It's the first end, you are throwing the yellow rocks, and you have the hammer. Blue draws the top of the button **(1)**. You can either hit it and, in theory, have no chance of scoring more than one, or you can throw the corner guard, leaving the blue rock in a dangerous position.

Why not do both? Try throwing hack weight at the rock on the button and roll to the side behind the tee line **(2)**. Invariably, Blue will hit your rock and end up taking its place on the 8-foot **(3)**. Now you throw the corner guard on the opposite side to the blue rock **(4)**. Blue now has the option of hitting or drawing; I have found that most teams in this situation draw around your corner guard to split the house **(5)**. You have now achieved what you wanted in the first place: a corner guard to use later and your opponent's rock behind the tee line to freeze to, and, most importantly, the dangerous rock moved away from the scoring area.

Try it! Somebody will fall for it. Having your opposition play around your corner guard is a good thing, allowing you the option of following them. Hitting rock **1** will send the message to your opponent that you are a defensive team until you score 3 points.

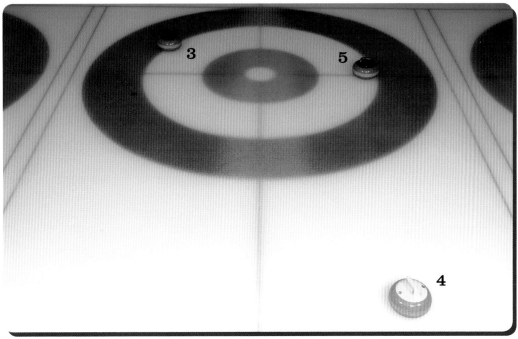

SCENARIO 13: ONE GOOD MISS DESERVES ANOTHER

Without the hammer, Blue throws a centre guard **(1)**. Yellow tries to come around, but misses short—the right way **(2)**. Blue counters with the perfect draw behind the centre guard **(3)**. Yellow attempts the come around tap back, but again misses the right way— wrecking the centre guard, opening up the front and raising rock **1** onto rock **2** into the rings. With two misses the right way, you've moved the centre guard to expose the shot rock, raised one of your yellow rocks into the ring, and rolled over into the corner guard position to be used later.

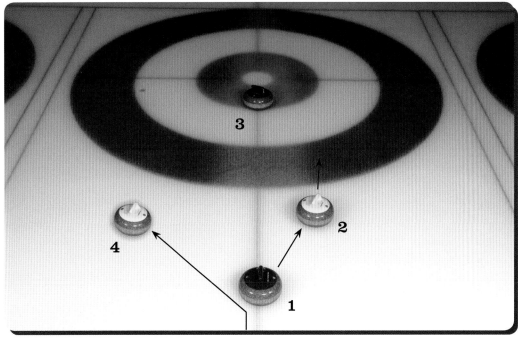

SCENARIO 14: APPROPRIATE WEIGHT

This time, you are Blue and are faced with a very thin double. Most curlers will throw peel weight at this shot. The problem with this is that if you hit the rock **3** slightly too thick, your shooter will roll over the top of the rock **2** and out into the open. There is an appropriate weight for each shot: in this case, try hack weight—there is much less chance of rolling out and giving Yellow the opportunity to bury a second rock. If you hit rock **3** a little too thick, your shooter will roll in front of the Yellow rock, behind cover—a smart miss.

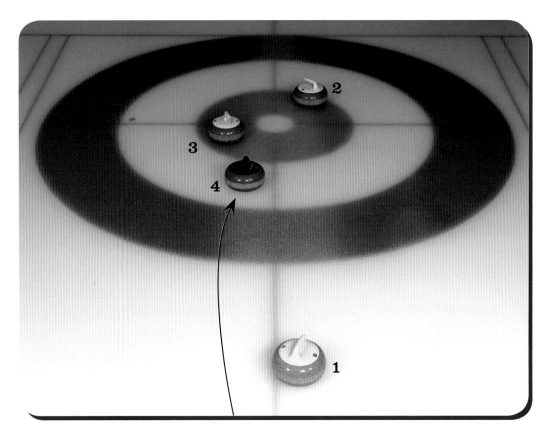

SCENARIO 15: PROPER ANGLES

This scenario is similar to Scenario 10. You are the blue team and have the hammer. Yellow is second shot rock (2), but you have a blue rock (3) frozen on an angle for shot rock. The play here would be a come-around draw (4) on the same side as rock 3, giving you the appropriate angle to raise rock 4 onto rock 3. If you can, bury only a small portion of rock 4—Yellow will have a very difficult time removing it without jamming it onto rock 3 and removing their own, leaving you sitting two and throwing for more. If Yellow elects to guard rock 3, you have the option of hitting rock 2 and sitting two or three. Always try to leave your team at least two options; your opponent can't cover two options with one guard.

SCENARIO 16: LINE THEM UP

The "double corner guard" means you (as Yellow) line up a second guard (**2**) directly in front of the first (**1**). It is nearly impossible to remove both of the guards and the shooter. If you get the chance, draw around to position **3**; Blue then removes one guard (**2**), and you draw to bury a rock (**5**). Now, the blue team is looking at two buried rocks and potentially giving up three.

SCENARIO 17: GET TO THE INSIDE

Blue has thrown the centre guard (**1**). Yellow has drawn around (**2**). Blue has countered with a freeze (**3**) that didn't quite curl enough to get directly in front of the yellow shot rock.

The trick here is to try to freeze your yellow rock (**4**) to the inside of the blue rock. The best leads in the country are very proficient at getting to the inside, which enables you to tap rock **4** onto rock **3** and remove it—or, if your opponent raises their blue guard onto the pile, rock **3** will leave the rings because of the favourable angle you created by getting to the inside.

SCENARIO 18: TOO GOOD TO BE TRUE

With the score tied and playing the ninth end without last rock, our team always throws the centre guard with our first rock **(1)**. If you throw it into the rings, you run the risk of a blank end. In this case, Blue has drawn to lie buried on the button **(2)**, which looks good on television but is actually a bad miss, since this allows Yellow to freeze on top of it **(3)**. Blue won't be able to move rock **3**, and will find it very difficult to score more than one. Yellow, meanwhile, has the option of raising rock **3** later in the end.

SCENARIO 19: DOMINATE THE SCORING AREA

With its first rock of the end, Yellow draws just outside the button **(1)**. You counter with a corner guard **(2)**. Yellow then guards its rock in the rings **(3)**. Your options are, apparently, to draw around or throw short. Give this a try: take less ice than needed for a draw to tick rock **3** over to the side and roll to position **4**. You now have three corner guards, and the shot rock **(1)** is exposed. More often than not, Yellow will respond by setting up another centre guard **(5)**. You then counter with a double on rocks **5** and **1**. *(Continued on page 108)*

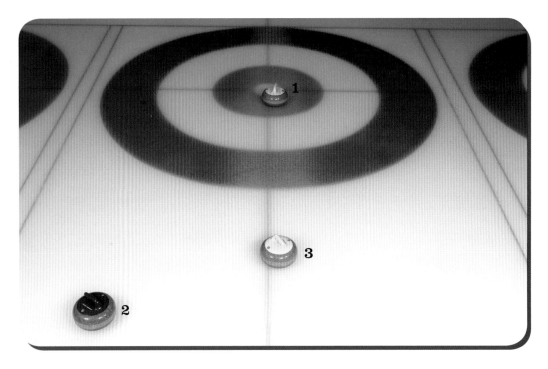

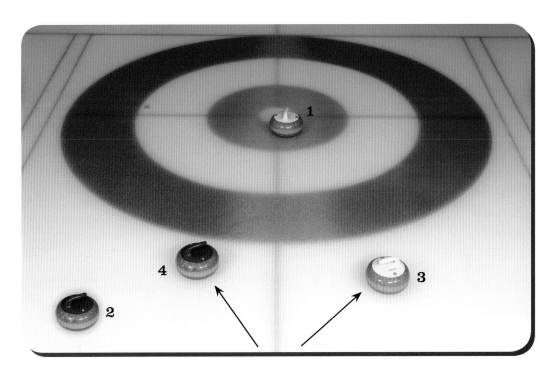

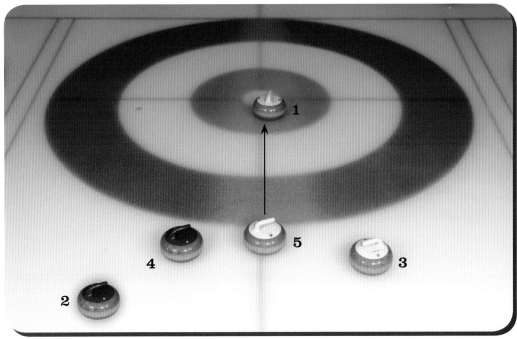

SCENARIO 19 (CONT'D)

Even if you remove only one of the yellow rocks, just as long as you stay out front **(6)**, you have control of the front with two very raisable rocks—meanwhile, the yellow rocks are off to the side, away from the scoring area. The key point here is to control the front—you don't have to be shot rock until the end is over!

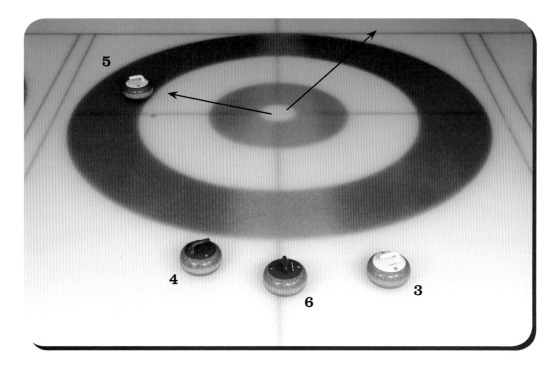

SCENARIO 20: MAKE THE OPPONENT'S ROCKS WORK FOR YOU

Just after the free guard zone came into effect, my team used this strategy a lot. Blue has thrown a centre guard **(1)**. Yellow draws short of the rings **(2)**. Blue, hoping to steal, draws around **(3)**. If you're Yellow, do not hit Blue **(3)** rock simply freeze in front of it; and you now have Blue covered on both sides.

TEAM BUILDING

PUTTING IT ALL TOGETHER

"I'm not looking for the best players. I'm looking
for the right players."
— Hockey coach Herb Brooks in the movie *Miracle*

I'VE ALWAYS FELT THAT CURLING is a unique sport because each member of the team contributes 25 per cent of the effort but has to do so 100 per cent of the time. There isn't room for a player to be less than fully prepared for all circumstances that might occur in the context of the game. Everyone delivers two rocks in each end, but there is no telling which player will be called upon to attempt the "key shot" (and in every game there is a key end, and in each end there is a key shot, and I'm amazed at how often the player who must deliver it is not

the skip). Some teams don't even have a coach to take that precious arm's-length view on key situations, and even when there is a coach, opportunities for dialogue with him or her are scarce. Curling is the ultimate team game.

TEAM CHEMISTRY

Team chemistry can be defined as a group dynamic that occurs when members of the team work together and make a united effort to accomplish the goals and objectives of the collective whole. Good chemistry can

I have seen a lot of less-talented teams beat much better squads because they had great team chemistry.

prevent the team from falling apart in times of great distress and turmoil, and can also be the "X factor" that propels a team to victory over an unevenly matched opponent.

I have seen a lot of less-talented teams beat much better squads because they had great team chemistry. There is also a lot to be said for wanting to win more than the other guy. Give me four athletes who are all pulling in the same direction and who share an intense desire to win, and I'll show you a club that is dangerous every time it hits the ice.

In 2000, Rick Perron, Wayne Tallon, Grant Odishaw, and I were members of a curling team that represented New Brunswick at the Brier in Saskatoon. Although we lost in the Brier final that year, I can vividly remember how proud I was of our team. New Brunswick had not previously been a major player at the Canadian championship, and we were absolute underdogs the entire week. But we had a team chemistry and a desire that were off the charts, and we beat teams that were supposed to dispose of us easily. Cohesiveness and desire can be your team's ace in the hole.

IMPROVING TEAM CHEMISTRY AND COHESIVENESS

Team chemistry and cohesiveness are qualities that you can develop. Here is a list of ways to make them valuable weapons in your team's arsenal.

• Learn to communicate effectively. Team chemistry demands that we invest as much time in communicating effectively as we do in our on-ice performance. Players have to feel comfortable expressing themselves frankly with the coach and with other members of the team. When I have been a skip, I've made it a point to make sure that all team members knew that their thoughts, opinions, suggestions, and criticisms were welcome at all times. Collaborate with the team to set specific and challenging goals for the upcoming season. When setting goals for the team, be smart. Set short- and long-term goals, and make sure they are measurable and realistic. Set realistic time frames for the achievement of each objective, so that you can gauge your progress. And don't just set these goals: have strategies in place

for how you plan to achieve them. Define
and delineate these goals clearly from
the outset, and make sure that each player
buys into the plan before proceeding—
ownership is key! If you look back at the
personal goals and the Team Gushue
goals set just before the 2005–06 season
(pages 48 and 49), I think you'll see that
they were smart, well thought out,
and, most important, achievable.

- Work to develop a sense of pride and
  shared identity. For a coach, this is a fine
  line to walk, but it can be done if you
  work to foster a climate of support
  between team members. Players need
  to feel that others on the team—coaches
  included—"have their back," but this
  trust will cease to develop if you don't
  work to provide consistent and contingent
  feedback to each athlete, regardless of
  skill level. Toby McDonald did a brilliant
  job of achieving this during our Olympic
  year. Individuals need to feel as though
  they are valuable and contributing
  members of the team.

- Be systematic in conducting both team
  and individual meetings throughout the
  course of the season. In all things be
  consistent—this was the hidden key
  to our success throughout our run to
  Olympic gold.

- Don't wait until a problem arises to
  conduct a meeting—by that time, it's too
  late. Work to minimize intra-team conflict
  by clearly defining individual roles, being
  honest and genuine in your communication, and providing constructive and
  relevant feedback where necessary.

- Let your skip be your guide in judging
  the climate of your team. A hot climate
  (indicated by bickering or arguing
  amongst teammates) or a cold one
  (where there is non-verbal dissension and
  unspoken conflict) will ruin any chance of
  developing a cohesive unit.

- Know your mates! Take the time to get to
  know your teammates as people and their
  lives outside of the sport. Athletes are not
  machines; they are human beings, and
  they have thoughts, feelings, and lives off
  the ice, just as you do.

ROLES AND RESPONSIBILITIES

Whether you're an experienced curler or
are new to the game, a better understanding of the roles and responsibilities of your
teammates is a key ingredient in a winning
team. I've asked some of Canada's best
curlers to provide some perspective on the
positions they play.

THE LEAD

BY

KELLY SCOTT

SCOTT TOURNAMENT OF HEARTS CHAMPION, 2006

GONE ARE THE DAYS of describing the lead on your curling team as "the one who carries the broom bag" or "the one who fills up all the water bottles"—or, for some teams, "the one who buys the drinks in the bar." These tasks apparently now fall to the skip! The lead position is the one that beginning curlers are often asked to play, but at the elite level, it can be one of the game's most challenging roles. You will often hear lead players express pride in their position, saying that they'd "rather be a lead on a great team than a skip on a half-decent team," or "rather be a great lead than an okay second." I couldn't agree more.

The lead position demands finesse, precision, extreme "feel," and incredible athletic ability. While the physical demands of sweeping six consecutive rocks per end are obvious to any onlooker, the position of lead also demands a great deal of concen-

tration and precise shot-making to set up the ends properly. The skip of the team, or the entire team as a whole, will likely have a strategic plan in mind for each end. It is up to the lead, with the help of the sweepers and the skip calling the ice, to ensure the plan's execution by putting the lead rocks in the exact locations specified. The lead's rock placement can dictate the outcome of an entire end strategy and can often be the deciding factor in wins or losses.

The lead position requires exceptional touch, and the free guard zone rule has added a whole new dimension to the game, demanding an even greater level of precision from the lead. When a team needs a guard to set up the end for stealing a point, the lead must deliver in order to take advantage of the free guard zone rule. When a team needs to draw around that guard to the button to steal a point, the lead sets this up. When a team needs to follow down an opposing team's rock, the lead needs to execute this delicate shot. And then there's the tick shot, a relatively new shot and a product of the free guard zone rule.

Lead rocks are often wide-open shots, made without many other rocks in play, but that doesn't reduce the importance of placement. If a guard is called, it must be placed in the exact spot called—in the free guard zone, placed according to where the curl happens (so that you can bury around the guard), close enough to the rings (so you can use the rock to run back later in the end and so that the skip can raise that rock to the button to score later in the end), and on and on. In particular, consider a situation where a team needs a guard to steal a point in the last end: if the first lead's rock slips into the rings and can be hit out of play, the opportunity to steal the winning point could be lost because of the first rock thrown in that end.

Often the lead's stones will be used as setup shots for the remaining six. When a freeze shot is called to an opponent's stone, it is crucial that this freeze remain in front of the opponent's rock so your team can later promote it. If this rock slips deep in the rings, it can sometimes be used to your detriment rather than your benefit later in the end. These are the rocks that we often refer to as the "control zone rocks," or the set-up rocks. Quite often, the lead rocks should be thrown to the sweepers, who can drag the rock a couple of extra feet if need be, rather than with the exact weight—because if sweeping is needed for line, then the rock will slip too deep to be useful.

Leads often joke about how they "throw two, sweep six, and keep their mouths shut." The two shots they throw to start off the end, and the six they sweep, all call for a great deal of concentration, and this focus is actually a point of pride for leads. Sweeping requires a great amount of physical exertion, but it also demands good judgment and split-second decision-making when it comes to how much pressure or friction to apply. A good sweeper is also diligent in making sure that the ice surface has been cleaned before a rock is thrown—another way the lead can contribute to the rest of the team's shots as the end unfolds. Add in the components of split timing, hog-to-hog timing, watching the thrower's speed out of the hack, relating that information to the feel she had when throwing her shots, and then judging the rocks as they travel down the sheet of ice—leads are a talented bunch! I have often observed the unique relationship—the strong bond and ability to communicate—between the top skips in our game and their leads. I think the best skips know just how good their leads can make them look!

It is quite evident when curling is shown on television, where the players are wearing microphones, how much a skip depends on the lead for feedback and communication. You need look no further than longtime duos such as Kevin Martin and Don Bartlett, Nancy Delahunt and Colleen Jones, and the contributions of Marcel Rocque to the entire Ferbey rink. Although communication is so important, it is equally, if not more, crucial to conduct dialogue at the right time and in the right way, so as not to distract the skip. Often, this communication occurs right before the skip throws her shots, so this communication style is a unique and informative one developed between the two players. Some skips look for final feedback from their players before throwing their rocks, and some skips prefer not to be distracted when they get to the hack to throw their shots. This element of the lead–skip relationship needs to be worked out to ensure maximum familiarity and optimal results.

Rocks thrown by the lead offer the skip a chance to get a good read on the sheet.

The lead might be called upon to throw a draw to the four-foot—a shot the skip will frequently need to play herself, seven rocks later, to score points for the team. Or a lead will throw a wide-open centre-line guard—a shot a skip might need to play to steal a point later in that same end. Another common shot for the lead is a wide-open nose hit on a four-foot rock—something the skip will throw to score a point at the conclusion of the end. The way these rocks behave can provide valuable information to the skip in terms of ice conditions as well as appropriate shots, turns, and weights to call for throughout the end. Sometimes, when a team is up several points and the objective is to keep the end clean, you'll see a skip ask the lead to throw the first rock of the end right through the house. Don't be fooled into thinking this is just a "wasted" shot. The skip is very closely watching the way this rock is thrown, so she can give the second, third, and skip the right ice to make the peels as the end unfolds. The lead needs to understand how important it is that she throw each shot straight, with the right weight, and as though it were the most important rock of that entire end.

Just as it is the lead's role to provide good reads on her rocks for the skip, it is also crucial for the lead to communicate the draw weight in certain paths on the sheet—again, these can often be the same paths that the skip will need to throw down with the final rocks of the end, and different paths can require different weights. The lead has the opportunity to throw open shots down these paths, and doing so can yield a great deal of insight into how the sheet of ice is reacting in different areas. Perhaps a lead might throw the first draw to the four-foot, after which the rest of the team's shots are hits and draws in the outside edges of the house, but the shot needed for the skip's final rock to score is that same draw to the centre four-foot circle. This is where the communication between skip and lead is crucial to the entire team's success. The lead and skip need to relate to the feel of the ice and throw the rocks in a similar way.

When you play in a 10-day round-robin event, rock matching is an important component. At the conclusion of the round robin, the top teams choose the set of rocks they want to play with during the playoff games. I believe our leads really can detect the slight similarities and differences in the way some rocks react, because they often throw many of the same draw shots during a game. Throwing open draws or hits offers a good opportunity to develop a sense of confidence with a consistent set of rocks.

The relationship between a lead and skip is evident once again when the lead passes on her "good set" of rocks to the skip to throw. While it used to be the case that the skip would reciprocate by passing her "bad rocks" down to the lead to throw, rock placement is now so important, thanks to the free guard zone rule, that the inconsistent rocks are now usually given to the second to throw, so as not to jeopardize the strategy of an entire end.

A strong lead player is a huge asset to any curling team. Leads work hard, are solid shooters, communicate their knowledge to the rest of the team, yet often have to stand back and remain quiet. They often instill confidence in the rest of the team by setting up the end well, and they take pride in how hard they will sweep their teammates' rocks to the exact positions required. Leads are the workhorses on our teams—who would certainly not be able to position the rocks as well as they can without the special contributions and talents of their leads!

THE SECOND

BY

MARK DACEY

BRONZE MEDALLIST, 2004 WORLD CURLING CHAMPIONSHIPS

THE POSITION OF SECOND requires a combination of great shot-making skills and a delicate balance of personnel management and strategy input. This position should not be looked upon lightly in the formation of any team with high aspirations.

To begin with, seconds must be able to deliver rocks with great speed and accuracy. With the free guard zone rule, which doesn't allow takeout shots until the fifth rock of the end, they occasionally find themselves in a less than desirable situation when called upon to deliver their first stone. In this case, it is a great asset to be able to get out of trouble with one great shot or a combination of two very good shots, such as double takeouts, runbacks, angle raise takeouts, and double peels. A second can turn a bad-looking end into a good-looking one—or at least allow some offensive manoeuvring to begin.

Alternatively, when an end has begun well, it is the second's duty to continue applying pressure. Well-positioned rocks will deny the opposing shooter the opportunity for the "out" shot. Positioning rocks well when a team is on the offence comes from a combination of delivering on an accurate line with a speed that gives the sweepers a chance to place it. Therefore, a great second will also have a delicate touch and feel for all the soft shots.

In terms of skill, great seconds are players who can throw the first stone a million miles per hour and move a ton of granite in all directions, and then come back on the second stone and draw the top of the four-foot with on-and-off sweeping. They don't waste a lot of time preparing for shots, but take calls quickly, throwing what the skip asks for. A skilled second will likely know the call before the opposition stone

A second can turn a bad-looking end into a good-looking one.

comes to rest, based on the simple premise of continuing with offence or looking for the "out."

The best seconds are usually great strategists as well. Without question, most tough decisions during a game are debated between the skip and third, but when they cannot agree, a front-end vote is often needed. This does not mean that the second is the front end's messenger by default: the second and the lead need to work as one, conducting their own discussion even as a potential strategy debate is developing, so that they can provide unified input if needed. A simple rule of thumb is that one front-end vote is better than two. (If the front end can't agree, then the team is still left without a firm decision.) Seconds should also be able to provide some input on the difficulty levels of shots if ice conditions are changing or becoming difficult. When ice in the scoring area becomes soft late in a game, it can be much easier to hit and stay on an open rock than draw to a spot with guesswork involved.

Seconds are generally skilled enough to skip, but often choose not to, because they understand the importance of their role. They prefer the "workhorse" job that comes along with front-end duties and aren't concerned that their names are not always in the limelight. They could easily make all the hard shots that skips are left to make, but when working with capable skips, they derive just as much satisfaction from sweeping rocks to their destinations. Seconds are consummate team players who have little or no interest in individual awards or recognition.

The best seconds in the game often play the role of "spark plug" or motivator, since they have the ability to recognize critical moments in the game and say what needs to be said. If the team is playing poorly, the second may need to light a fire under the rest of the team to get them going. When the skip is about to deliver an important shot, the ideal second will make a positive comment such as "Nail this one" or "This is your shot" before the delivery of the stone. Skilled seconds make comments like this, even when not confident with the call or the ice, because they recognize the importance of positive reinforcement. Conversely, poor seconds will point out possible negative outcomes or suggest other options, creating doubt in the minds of their skips.

Off the ice, great seconds will accept some of the responsibilities that come along with the organization of a team or the logistics of its season. Arranging sponsorships, hotel bookings, airline bookings, submitting entries, and co-ordinating clothing and equipment are just some of the tasks seconds may take on. Often, they enjoy organizing the broom handles, broom heads, gloves and so on, since, along with their front-end partners, seconds bear the brunt of the sweeping.

Seconds have extensive knowledge of the impact that sweeping has on stones, sweeping styles, and brush and ice conditions. This player will often carry a "rock book" and note anything relevant that might come up during a game. Seconds will be able to provide input on rock selection, and the team's history with each type, before any game. A second often gets stuck with any "bad" stones that the rest of the team cannot use, since the lead needs to have a nice set for draw weight, and the skip definitely needs a matched set. The best seconds relish this challenge. They continually remind their skips, when calling shots, which rock is being thrown and advise them to ice or call "sweep" as appropriate.

Lastly, the ideal second is someone who plays the game for the love of the sport and has high aspirations. Like the rest of the team, this player has very clear goals and realizes that they cannot be accomplished alone or without sacrificing time, energy, money, or whatever else is necessary. The best seconds are fun to play with but can be intense and demanding—but only because they want to succeed so badly that they are completely focused on the goal.

THE THIRD

BY

WADE BLANCHARD

SKIP, TEAM NEW BRUNSWICK, 2005 TIM HORTONS BRIER

EVERY POSITION ON A CURLING TEAM is important, but the third, sometimes called the "vice" or "mate," can be the most important position on the team as well as the most enjoyable one to play. Thirds have opportunities to play wonderful shots, sweep, call line on the skip's shots, help with strategic decision-making, and much, much more. Let's take a look at this position and some of the qualities that make a good third.

Big Shooter. The third on most successful competitive teams is the best all-around shooter on the team. The four-rock free guard zone rule means that the second is playing more draw shots. If the end is setting up in the opponent's favour, the third must be able to make the big bail shot. Having a third who can make that big freeze, hit and roll, or run through at just the right time can save, or even win, a lot of ends for

a team. And a third who can play the "high hard" shot with pinpoint accuracy is a great weapon for any team; his skill can make the difference between stealing and giving up a big end.

Communicator. The third is the liaison between the front end and the skip, and must be able to pass information back and forth when necessary. Sometimes this involves defusing any potential problems before they escalate to derail the team. It's the third's responsibility to make sure that the skip is aware of changing ice conditions or of any rocks that react differently (i.e., ones that curl more, move slower, faster, straighter, etc.). When calling line, a good third knows when to change the call in mid-shot and go to Plan B if the original call is not going to work. When there is a time limit, the third can ensure that nobody is wasting time, making certain, for instance, that the front

121

end is already in the hack when the skip is ready to make the call, so that the back end has more time if a strategy discussion is needed. Sometimes, the skip will make changes to the game plan decided upon in the pre-game meeting, and in this case, the a good third will make sure that the front end is aware of the new strategy and on the same page as the skip. (Front ends nowadays know the game well and are very capable of helping with strategy calls, but if skips are getting advice from everyone on their teams, they may become uncertain, and the result may be disagreement as well as wasted time on the clock.)

Cheerleader. I don't mean get out your pompoms; most thirds have better ways to encourage their teammates. It's important that they keep everything positive, and don't let misses cause their teams to lose focus. Some players aren't focused enough, while others are too focused or uptight, and it's the third's job to identify each and react accordingly. On one occasion, for instance, I was playing third for Charlie Sullivan Jr.—a very accomplished third, but a relatively new skip, Charlie had just missed an easy and important shot, and our opponents stole the end. We could all see that Charlie was very embarrassed and upset with himself, and it was my job to get him back on track. After sweeping the lead's rock down at the beginning of the next end, I went back and stood beside Charlie. After a few seconds, I turned and asked him if he needed a hug. Well, a big smile came across his face, he replied with a quick "no!" and I told him to forget about it and move on. He did, and we then proceeded to win our way right to the final.

Supporter. After skipping for most of my curling career, I have come to believe that a supportive third is worth his weight in gold. All teams get along when they're winning, but the best teams know how to support each other during rough times. Without the third's support, any skip can go into the tank in the blink of an eye. It's important for a third to understand the game that is being called and believe in that game, but equally so to provide other options as they come up or the need arises. Once all the options have been provided and the skip has chosen the shot, a good third makes sure that the skip knows that he is supporting his decision. Criticizing strategy is easy for those who don't have to throw the final brick, but one negative comment can tear down what it took six months to build up. It is up to the third to be confident in agreeing with the ice call or suggesting it might not be quite the right ice for the shot. As well,

A third can make or break a team. It is essential that thirds know and understand their position on their teams.

if the front end makes errors in judgment while sweeping, it's important to respect their decisions and learn how the mistake can be fixed. The only truly bad decision is no decision at all. After lots of hard work and practice, everyone on the team has the same goal—to play the best they can and win the game or the bonspiel. Mistakes will be made, but the team must learn to overcome them and move on—sometimes easier said than done.

A third can make or break a team. It is essential that thirds know and understand their position on their teams. If a third is thinking, "I should be calling the game" or "I should be throwing the last rock," the skip can sense this lack of support and lose confidence—and then the whole team suffers.

Behind every great team is a great third who knows the importance of his position. If you can handle all of this and come to play on Sunday, you can be a great third!

THE SKIP

BY

RUSS HOWARD

THE SKIP IS NOT THE MOST IMPORTANT position. In fact, many a great quartet has gone by the wayside with a skip who believes his role is the most important.

One of a skip's primary roles is to involve the entire team in identifying the team's goals. This discussion between the four team members could include things like time off work, family commitments, planning a bonspiel schedule, clarifying what tasks each player will have off the ice—for example, booking plane tickets, hotel rooms, and transportation, cresting the sweaters, submitting entries, arranging for sponsors, and setting the budget. It is amazing how many teams at this level are on a different page when it comes to the off-ice decisions.

There is a lot more to the role of the skip than just throwing the last two rocks and barking out orders. Over the years, I have learned that it is vitally important for the team to get along both on and off the ice. It is imperative that the team bonds—whether through getting together for pizza, team practices, playing pool or cards during an event, or what have you.

It is a huge benefit if all players can get together for regular practices. This allows time to work on identified problems, play two-on-two games, or work on particular shots. We focus on practices that are competitive to ensure we all stay sharp. Another thing we work on is practising without a stopwatch. I am a firm believer that players get lazy when they use a stopwatch. Everyone on the team needs to concentrate on the path of each rock and the changes in the ice conditions as the game progresses. This will improve each player's "touch."

I find that, as a skip, I spend as much time as I can watching my teammates, looking

It is vitally important for the team to get along both on and off the ice.

for slight irregularities and patterns that might help me put the broom in the right spot for each. In the fall of 2006, I had very little time to prepare for the Olympic trials. Our lead, Jamie Korab, had a very soft out-turn release, plus he drifted slightly left. This caused Jamie's out-turn to curl six to seven inches more than that of the rest of the team. As I explained to Jamie, this was not a problem; in fact, it would become our secret weapon. Every chance we got, I called for the out-turn come-around, allowing six or seven more inches of ice, and Jamie, because of his wonderful touch (without a stopwatch!), put us in a positive situation time and time again. It made it very difficult for the opposition to re-create Jamie's out-turn. The old golf adage comes to mind: it's not how, it's how many. Jamie was smart enough to continue to throw the rock differently from the rest of us; he resisted the urge to change his release to emulate the others'. Borrowing from golf again, if you slice the ball and it ends up in the middle of the fairway, do it again on the second hole!

At an elite level, any player can be the best player on the team. One of the skip's jobs is to make sure there are no egos and no hidden agendas. Over the years, I found that my attitude on and off the ice directly affected the entire team's performance. I felt that my role at the Olympic trials was to keep the boys in a calm and focused state. There are a lot of great curlers who can make a high percentage of the shots; the question is whether they can be in the mental position to make the high percentage of shots when they really have to.

One of the main roles of the skip is to identify the team's strengths and weaknesses and call the game accordingly. I'm also a firm believer in accepting input from teammates. When I have to throw an important shot, I have the luxury of calling the amount of ice and the desired weight for my shot. Why not extend this courtesy to the other members of the team when you can for some of their shots?

Media attention is generally focused around the skip. Most curlers will say that the skip is either the hero or the goat. It

There are a lot of great curlers who can make a high percentage of the shots; the question is whether they can be in the mental position to make the high percentage of shots when they really have to.

may seem that the skip ends up with an undue share of the accolades. It is up to the skip to reinforce to their mates, as well as to the media, that winning—or losing—is a team effort. The skip also has to walk a fine line with the team when quotes are taken out of context. This is another reason why good communication within the team is vitally important.

Attitude is the key. Enjoy the game, and curl with teammates who love the game as much you do!

THE FIFTH

BY

TOBY McDONALD

TEAM CANADA COACH, 2006 OLYMPIC GAMES

WHAT DO YOU WANT in a fifth player? What is the role of a fifth player? How a team goes about addressing these questions will influence its chances for success.

A team needing a fifth person is generally playing at an elite level, and the player they seek will need to be a permanent team member, not just a spare to be called up regularly to fill in. Whether it's for an event, a series of events, or a season, this player is considered permanent for that time.

Before there is any bantering about who potential candidates might be, the whole team must first think and talk about what they are looking for in the player. In the case of the Brad Gushue team, when we were looking for a fifth in the lead-up to the Olympic trials, we agreed that our ideal fifth needed to do the following:

(1) fit into the present team dynamic

(2) be a good player

(3) buy into the team's training, practice, and playing schedule

(4) buy into the team's sports psychology

(5) be able to throw from third position down

(6) be mature

(7) not be a distraction

(8) not have an alarmist or pessimistic personality

(9) support team decisions

(10) have experience in Trials-like settings

(11) add something to the team

(12) do whatever he could to help the team

(13) be happy with the fifth position

The majority of these items would likely apply to any team looking for a fifth, but the list may be added to or subtracted from to reflect the team's specific requirements or the event they're preparing for. In the case of the Gushue team, requirement number 5 was initially specific, as we felt that, if Brad couldn't play, Mark Nichols, who had just won the National Mixed as a skip, would fill his position. At that point, we did not know what the final lineup would ultimately be.

Having developed and fine-tuned the list of requirements, we then turned to consider who could best fulfill the role. Under the circumstances, we initially thought that we could really consider every player in Canada who had not qualified for the Olympic trials (or already been picked up as a fifth man). This would have generated a long list of possibilities. But we soon found that, once we started considering specific individuals and discussing who could meet most of our requirements, the list shortened fairly quickly.

Obviously, most teams will never have the opportunity to select a Russ Howard. The point is that you need to know what you're looking for before you determine who it will be.

Once the player has been selected, the team, as formerly constituted, has changed: another personality has been added to the mix. It is important that the player and the team focus on a smooth transition. If the team has selected wisely, the transition period should proceed smoothly, but all team members have to be aware that some change is inevitable, and they should not resist it. The first thing that the team should do is provide the fifth with a copy of the list of requirements, so that he is aware of what characteristics and factors it considers important. This tell the fifth that the team chose him with care and that he wasn't picked just to carry the broom bags.

There's one more item that could be added to the requirements list: Once selected as a team member, the fifth will need to prove you made the right decision. He must ensure that he is fit and ready to play; he must try to get up to speed by practising with the team; he must play in and view team games; he must learn the team's strengths and weaknesses and help add to the former and reduce the latter. He must add as much value as he can.

In the case of the Gushue Olympic Trials Team, Russ Howard obviously brought a lot to the table with him. You don't get to six Canadian Finals without picking up a wee bit of game. On the other hand, his sweeping was, shall we just say, a little suspect. One immediate consideration the now-extended team needed to address was what position Russ would play if called upon. Brad is just great at throwing that last rock, so it was ultimately decided that if Russ

You need to know what you're looking for in a fifth before you determine who it will be.

were to play, he would hold the broom. As a result, Brad Gushue had to sweep for the first time since the age of 14 (a smooth transition that he has been given little credit for). Another immediate change that was made was that, as coach, I no longer held the broom for team practices. Russ needed to hold the broom to learn everybody's release and throwing tendencies.

In terms of setting out the roles that a fifth player can fulfill, I will use Mike Adam as an example. There is no better. Mike supported the team's decisions and fit in with the team's dynamic. He was a great player—fit, ready to play, and focused on the task at hand, he proved his worth when called on to play, particularly in the Olympic semi-final game against the United States. Out of the limelight, he not only tracked and recorded all rocks, attended to any item that could have been a distraction to the rest of the team, and advised and assisted the coach on everything, but also made everyone laugh and helped them stay relaxed.

He "sucked it up," as our team performance mentor, Marnie McBean, suggested we would all have to do. Accepting the role he was ultimately asked to play, he was an integral part of the team's ultimate success and stands as a beacon for fifth players worldwide.

MENTAL TOUGHNESS

IT'S ALL IN THE MIND

"I'm about five inches from being an outstanding golfer.
That's the distance my left ear is from my right ear."
— BEN CRENSHAW

HOW DO YOU REGAIN YOUR FOCUS for a crucial shot in the 10th if you've just blown a gimme in the previous end? How will you be able to maintain a high level of confidence in your ability when you've been mired in a slump for an extended period of time? How do you overcome the feeling of intimidation when facing a much better opponent? How do you overcome the fatigue factor when you've played four must-win games in two days?

These are just some of the situations that test our mental toughness and our individual will to win. Mental toughness, or the lack thereof, has been both an asset and a detriment to my game over the years.

Again, I go back to the fact that I am from the old school. In my youth, mental toughness was seen as something you either had or you didn't. Trial and error, winning and losing were the things that made you smarter, tougher, and mentally strong, and it didn't take long to determine which opponents were mentally tough and which ones were soft.

So what does it mean to be mentally

tough, anyway? For some, it means being able to overcome injury, pain, or discomfort and "gut it out." It's sort of a badge of honour. To others, being mentally tough is about dealing successfully with pressure and finding a way to overcome fear or worry. Still others see mental toughness as the ability to embrace hard work and to set and meet high standards for oneself. For me, mental toughness encompasses all of these elements.

BEATING A BETTER OPPONENT OR TEAM

Perhaps the greatest test of mental toughness comes from facing an opponent who is "better"—more successful or more experienced—than your team. Imagine stepping onto the ice at the Brier or Tournament of Hearts for the first time and knowing that you have to face Randy Ferbey or Colleen Jones. It is easy to be intimidated or overwhelmed by opponents who are vastly more experienced, but you can still win.

How? By using your mind, playing smarter than them. By learning to become opportunistic. No matter how great your opponent is, there are always scoring opportunities in a game. Your mission is to seize these opportunities and exploit the openings your opponent gives you. On the flip

side, you must learn to limit the number of mistakes you make and use your focus and concentration to reduce the number of chances for your opponent. While it is true that mistakes are a part of the game, you can be assured that if you're playing an elite team and you keep offering up chances for them to score, eventually it will come back to haunt you. Be confident and call upon the self-discipline derived from your hours of practice. Use your knowledge of strategy and tactics to devise winning game plans and win every game you can!

COPING WITH ADVERSITY

If you play this sport long enough, it is inevitable that you will face moments of adversity. It has been my experience that the longer you play, the less afraid you become of facing moments of self-doubt. To most athletes, the word "adversity" conjures up visions of failure, losing, and other very negative images that need to be avoided at all costs. I have found, through decades of play, that adversity can ultimately be a very positive experience if you can see it for what it is.

I have certainly endured my share of losing as well as winning. I have played in games where I have cost my team the opportunity to win, blown big shots at the

"You learn you can do your best, even when it's hard. Even when you're tired and maybe hurting a little bit. It feels good to show some courage." —JOE NAMATH, legendary NFL quarterback

most inopportune time, seen my confidence dip to a level where I thought I would not play well again, and seen my enthusiasm for the game disappear to the point where coming to the rink wasn't fun anymore. When you've played this game as long as I have, you begin to realize that peaks and valleys are as much a part of the game as ice and rocks.

The key to overcoming adversity is to try not to overreact to the situation. When facing a difficult situation, try to take a step back and look for a way to turn what is seemingly a no-win situation into a positive and defining moment.

In 1987 I faced one of those moments at the World Championships in Vancouver. In the Brier final that year, our team, representing Ontario, had played almost flawlessly en route to a hard-fought victory over a very tough Bernie Sparkes team from British Columbia. It was a tremendous feeling to know that we had won a tough national championship, and an even greater thrill to have the opportunity to don the maple leaf at the World Championships for the very first time.

It didn't take long, however, for our enthusiasm to be tempered somewhat, as the ice conditions on Opening Day turned out to be a lesson in the importance of being able to overcome difficulty. Our first-round matchup against France looked to be, for all intents and purposes, a gimme, and for the first half of the game it was. We executed our game plan to perfection and raced to a 5–1 lead by the midpoint of the match. However, B.C. Place, the host venue for the championships, threw us a curveball that instantly turned our fortunes around.

B.C. Place, a domed stadium, has a Teflon roof, which can turn the building into a bit of a greenhouse when the sun is strong. From the first end through the fifth, the ice conditions were nearly perfect, and our shot-making ability overwhelmed France.

But then the heat inside the stadium took its toll on the ice, and our sheet slowed considerably. We hogged an unbelievable 19 rocks in the second half of the game and lost 7–6 to France. Losing a key first draw we should have won was bad enough; but to add insult to injury, as our game went south a number of fans began to chant, "Where's Bernie?" —a not-so-veiled reference to B.C.'s native son.

In a postgame interview, I mentioned the ice conditions and suggested that it might be a good idea to move the afternoon matches to later in the day in order to help maintain good ice. It seemed like a perfectly sensible suggestion to me. As it turned out, a local newspaper interpreted my suggestion as a sign of poor sportsmanship. The headline in the next morning's paper read "Howard #1 Complainer." In less than 24 hours, we had gone from the euphoria of representing Canada in the biggest event in the sport to losing a round-robin game we should have won and becoming the target of derision by a segment of our own fans.

It seemed obvious to me at that point that our inaugural appearance at the World Championships could go one of two ways: we could feel sorry for ourselves, fold under the mounting pressure, and have our first World Championships become an unmiti-gated disaster; or we could come together as a team and find a way to put that experience behind us and come out determined to play better. We chose the latter. We came back that night to B.C. Place and tried to figure out what had happened. After throwing some rocks right to the four-foot circle, I began to realize that it might not be the ice that was to blame; it was the rocks. The sun had been heating the rocks up, reducing the distance they would slide and making them very inconsistent. We quickly devised a foil covering to protect our rocks.

We also came back together as a team. We beat Eigil Ramsfjell from Norway, the pre-tournament favourite, in a must-win situation in the second draw, which acted as a catalyst for the rest of the week, as we won our first world championship.

If there is a lesson here, it is that adversity need not be something to fear or shy away from. Instead, embrace it, recognize it for what it is, and allow it to make you and your team stronger. Even 20 years later, when the going gets tough, I still draw upon that experience in Vancouver to help me.

ALL TEAMS ARE NOT CREATED EQUAL

Some teams are clearly better than others. They get more done, and with less squabbling. Still, there are instances of teams performing heroically, even though the members detest each other. In the 1970s, the Oakland Athletics of Reggie Jackson, Sal Bando, Joe Rudi, and Rollie Fingers were infamous for personality conflicts outside the foul lines; but on the diamond they were like a well-oiled machine that rolled its way to three consecutive World Series titles.

Of course, there are only a few teams that can have this degree of discord and still execute and win games on a regular basis. Ideally, you need to find curling mates who have the same goals and objectives that you do and who are willing to work towards a common goal. Not everyone can lead, but you should have a chemistry that will help you overcome the hard times, celebrate the good times, and make winning and getting better your main purpose for playing.

All teams experience conflict. The successful ones manage it and succeed in spite of it. I can't recall ever being a member of a team that had four or five athletes with similar attitudes, temperaments, and talent. In fact, I'm not sure that I would want to play on a team where there were no differences in style or approach. Successful teams manage to blend all styles and honour the differences so that the collective energies and capabilities are enhanced. A good

example can be found in the role I played in the 2006 Olympic trials with Brad Gushue. I was used to playing a very aggressive game, controlling the front and usually trying to leave tough finesse shots for the opposition. Brad, being younger, was capable of playing both styles, but with Mark Nichols at vice, they tended to try to be left with some big-weight shot to decide the end. I decided, after seeing our strengths and weaknesses as a team, that our best opportunity was to do a bit of both styles—our lead and I would set up the ends playing aggressive finesse shots, hopefully making and missing the right way, leaving Mark some short run-backs, which were his forte. All teams have weaknesses. The successful ones minimize these and play to their strengths to succeed.

CHECK YOUR EGO AT THE DOOR

One of Olympic coach Toby McDonald's favourite lines was "Check your egos at the door, boys." The fact that Brad Gushue relinquished the skip's role to me, and that for the first time in my career someone else was throwing the last two rocks of the end, is a testament to the importance of Toby's instruction. The same is true of some of the best teams in the world. Wayne Middaugh and Peter Corner made a choice to play front end for Glenn and me for five

"I drew my strength from fear. Fear of losing. I don't remember the games I won, only the games I lost."

—**BORIS BECKER,** three-time Wimbledon champion and the youngest-ever Wimbledon men's singles champion

years to help form a great team. John Morris left a very successful skipping career to play third for Kevin Martin. As Kent Carstairs, my longtime lead of 17 years, would say when asked why he didn't skip his own team, "I'd rather be the lead on a winning team than be the skip of a losing team." Or look at Mike Adam, the second on the Gushue team, who graciously stepped aside so I could play on the Olympic team. As the Toronto Star stated, this was one of the most unselfish acts in Canadian sports history. Successful teams do what they have to do to meet their goals. Egos only get in the way.

TEAM PROBLEMS DEMAND TEAM SOLUTIONS

There are times when modelling mental toughness is an individual thing, and then there are times when it is done as a team.

During the early stages of the preliminary rounds at the Olympics, our team was really firing on all cylinders—we were making all

the right calls and nailing all the big shots on the way to a 4–1 won-lost record that included wins over pre-tournament favourites Great Britain, Switzerland, and the defending Olympic gold medallist, Pal Trulsen of Norway.

In curling, though, momentum can swing at a moment's notice, and before we knew it we were looking at a 4–3 mark, including a stunning 7–6 extra-end loss to Italy. To say we were in a precarious position is an understatement; we were clinging to hopes of a playoff spot, and we needed to take immediate action.

At a team meeting held before our second-to-last round-robin game, which had become a must-win against New Zealand, we started to examine our situation and decide on a plan to turn this stressful period into our defining Olympic moment. Actually, our answer to our malaise was quite simple: we needed to relax, allow ourselves to have fun again, and allow our talent and skill to take over—in other words, we needed to stop thinking and just play.

The solution to our problem may have seemed quite obvious and quite simple, but if one player had tried to force this solution upon the rest of us, it would have been a big mistake. Our play and our approach to the tournament was a team problem, and because we came together as a team to find a solution, each player had ownership and everyone left that meeting feeling good about the direction we were taking to get back on track. We beat New Zealand 9–1 in our next game, and we were unstoppable after that, going 3–0 and winning the gold with a 10–4 win over Finland.

WANT TO WIN, BUT HATE LOSING

Tennis legend Billie Jean King said, "A champion is afraid of losing. Everyone else is afraid of winning." I hate losing, and anyone who has seen me play will tell you that this is true. I remember Denis Potvin, the great New York Islanders defenceman, once saying that he feared losing, that he feared looking bad, that he feared getting hurt, and that he feared being embarrassed on the ice. I share those same fears. I want to win every end, every game, every tournament. I don't think you need to carry it that far in order to get better, but you need to have the desire to win. Wanting to win is a positive

desire, while wanting to avoid losing is a negative one. Pick your poison. You have to know what motivates you to drive you towards your goals.

STAY MOTIVATED TO SUCCEED RIGHT UP TO THE END

You must make a conscious resolution to finish what you start. There will always be obstacles and roadblocks on the way to getting better and winning on a consistent basis, but you need to promise yourself that you will pick yourself up each and every time and keep striving towards your objectives. Almost without exception, the road to becoming a better curler is dotted with failure. You may be a novice who is beginning to see real improvement in your game, and then—boom!—you hit the wall and your shot-making goes south or your sweeping technique hits a snag. Good— that's the way it's supposed to be. Keep going, because hard work will turn things around eventually.

DON'T FEEL SORRY FOR YOUR OPPOSITION

Your opponents come to the competition of their own free will. Playing well and executing to the best of your ability is not something that you can turn on and off like a switch. You can't say to yourself, "Oh well, we're playing a weaker team today, so we'll play down to their level so as not to embarrass them—and then we'll turn it back on next game." It just doesn't work that way. You need to play your best at all times, because slumps and downturns will come on their own without your help. You cannot feel sorry for your opponent; nor can you worry about their performance. You must worry only about your own performance.

HAVING A COMPETITOR'S MINDSET DOES NOT MAKE YOU A BAD PERSON

You can be highly competitive, have a competitor's mindset, and still be an honest, fair, ethical sportsperson when you compete. But you can't control the opinion others hold of you. At the 2005 Nokia Brier, the Randy Ferbey rink had to endure heckling during the championship game against Mark Dacey. It was an unfortunate situation, but something that many teams have faced with a growing number of spectators. I came to the conclusion a long time ago that I couldn't control what others thought of me or my approach to the game, but what I could control was my approach to winning and getting better. For you, a stronger and more successful approach to the game probably means doing what you have to do, fairly

and ethically, and letting the chips fall where they may.

MENTAL TOUGHNESS UNDER PRESSURE

The key to being mentally tough is to make a commitment to perform high-quality work from start to finish. There is a tendency to rush into practising and playing without having first learned the individual skills. Like golf, curling is about technique, and you cannot take a shortcut when it comes to learning the proper way to make shots, sweep, or call a game. Take the time to create good habits and make them a part of your daily routine, so that you begin to execute them without even thinking.

Our opponent at the 1993 World Championships was David Smith from Scotland. We were winning 5–4 and had last shot in the crucial ninth end. Our team had played a great ninth end and we were sitting three rocks without any guards for the Scots to hide behind, when Smith threw his last rock. David threw a desperation freeze to the face of our shot rock on the button. This left me with an exacting takeout, having to hit a little less than half of his rock and spill it off our own to score at least three points, which would secure the victory with a four-point lead. I remember that my mindset at the time was focused on all the factors it would take to make this shot. In a club game, this isn't the most impossible shot in the world, but this particular shot was much more difficult than it looked. We were using very smooth, straight rocks. The arena was built for hockey, and the floor was tilted for drainage. To make the rink level, there were 13 inches of ice at one end of the sheet and less than one inch at the other end. At the "deep end," the surface of the ice was very warm and slippery, while at the "shallow end" the lack of ice made that surface too cold, creating frost and very different playing conditions. To add to the difficult situation, the sheet was also not level from side to side.

This particular shot was to be taken down the middle of the sheet, and we needed roughly six inches of negative ice, which forced me to put the broom in the middle of the rock, which was the only spot where I couldn't hit the rock. Mentally, I couldn't let myself be distracted by this broom position; I had to believe the rock would fall. My brother Glenn and I really had to talk about this shot and reassure ourselves that the rock would fall and that we both had the same expectation of how the rock would react.

I slid to the far end to prepare for my shot. Wayne and Pete, like any great front end, reassured me with positive comments like "Don't worry about it, Skipper, we'll sweep it and it will fall back." After all of the distractions had been cleared from my mind, everything had been simplified to the point that all I had to do was execute the shot by throwing the right weight and hitting the broom—just like I would in a club game. I've hit the broom a million times in games and in practice, and there was no reason in my mind why I couldn't do it again. I didn't allow my attention to drift to wondering what if I made this shot and won the world championship or—worse—what if I missed this shot and lost the world championship. Staying focused on the shot and staying in my routine was crucial for my self-confidence and for eventually making the shot.

For me, being mentally prepared at the time when you need it most—a time when you can eliminate the distractions and focus on throwing the right weight and hitting the broom with a seemingly impossible shot—comes from practice and mental toughness. When you're prepared and focused, you have the luxury of not feeling nervous, and you'll be a winning curler.

GLOSSARY

ANGLE
The position of a rock or shot relative to the sidelines and centre line of the sheet.

BACK LINE
A line running across the back of the house. A rock over the back line is out of play, but a rock touching it is still in play. The back line may also be used as a reference point for how hard to throw a rock—as in "Throw back-line weight" for a rock to travel to the very back of the house.

BITER
Any rock that touches at the edge of the 12-foot circle and is therefore in play and eligible to score. Under the four-rock rule, any of the first four rocks thrown may be measured to determine whether it is biter. In all other cases, measuring devices of any kind can be used only after completion of the end.

BITER STICK
A metal rod exactly six feet long, used to measure whether or not a rock is a biter (in the house).

BLANK END
An end in which neither team scores a point, after which there is no change in the order in which the teams throw the first and last rocks of the next end. Sometimes a team will intentionally blank an end to retain the last-rock advantage in the next end.

BONSPIEL

An organized curling event consisting of several games.

BROOM (OR BRUSH)

The device used to sweep the path of a moving rock.

BRIER

The Canadian men's national championship, held annually since 1927. Since its inception, its sponsors have been Macdonald Tobacco, Labatt Breweries, Nokia, and Tim Hortons.

BURNED ROCK

A rock touched, by any part of a player or his equipment, while it is moving. Burned rocks must be removed from play. The non-offending skip can allow the play to stand or place the touched rock and all the rocks that were affected back in their original positions.

BUTTON

The one-foot circle in the centre of the house. In televised competitions, the button may be two feet in diameter to allow space for a sponsor's name.

"CAN'T HURT IT!"

Advice to sweepers to continue sweeping because it will do no harm and may help the outcome.

CASHSPIEL

A curling tournament (bonspiel) where curlers compete for prize money.

CENTRE LINE

A line marked down the middle of the ice sheet, from hack to hack.

CORNER GUARD

A rock in front of the house and off to one side that protects another rock or part of the house.

COUNTER

A rock that is closer to the centre of the house than any opponent's rock and is therefore a potential point.

CURL

The distance a curling rock curves off a straight line when thrown.

DELIVERY BALANCE DEVICE

An alternative to a broom or brush used to help stay balanced during delivery. Often called a "crutch," the delivery balance device is usually made from plastic tubing and is held with a player's free hand while he or she throws a rock.

DELIVERY STICK

A stick or brush handle that slips over the handle of a rock, permitting a player to deliver a rock from a standing position.

DOUBLE

When two rocks are removed from play.

DRAW (SHOT)

A shot that stops in a selected area without the objective of touching another rock.

DRAW WEIGHT

The momentum required for a rock to reach a target.

END

The portion of a curling game that is completed when both teams have thrown all their rocks and the score has been decided. Games are normally eight ends in club play and 10 ends in competitive play. An extra end may be needed to resolve a tie.

FALL

A rock that, because of ice conditions, curves in the opposite direction to what was intended. For example, an out-turn thrown with the right hand should curve to the left. If ice conditions cause it to curve to the right, this is called a fall. (See also negative ice.)

FIFTH-END BREAK

In 10-end competitive curling, a five-minute rest period customarily held at the end of the fifth end of play.

FIFTH (PLAYER)

An alternate player.

FOUR-FOOT

The smallest ring in the house, outside the button, with a diameter of four feet.

FREE GUARD ZONE

The area between the hog line and the tee line, excluding the house.

FREEZE

A draw where the delivered rock comes to rest touching another rock without moving it. If it is not directly in front of the rock it is touching, it is called an angle freeze.

GRIPPER

A slip-on cover for a curling shoe, which gives a sweeper better traction when he or she is moving down the ice.

GUARD

A rock placed in a position to protect another rock or part of the playing area.

HACKS

Foot holds, a pair of which are located at each end of the ice (one on either side of the centre line), used to push off during delivery of the rock. Left-handed players place their left foot in the right hack, while right-handed players put their right foot in the left hack; this helps ensure that all rocks are delivered approximately down the centre line.

HACK (WEIGHT)

Force with which a rock must be thrown in order to reach the hack at the far end of the ice.

HAMMER

The right to throw the last rock of an end, given to the team that lost the previous end. A team may choose not to score in an end in order to keep the hammer in the next one.

HEAVY

Thrown too hard; overthrown.

HIT

The opposite of a draw: a shot that strikes another rock, thus causing its removal from the playing area.

HITTING THE BROOM

Throwing the rock accurately, so that it reaches the target set by the skip or vice. (The skip or vice usually indicates a target with his/her broom or brush.)

"HURRY HARD!"

A plea to sweep with greater effort. Skips have been known to yell this phrase extremely loudly, and quite frequently, as the rock travels down the ice. If you yell this correctly, you can intimidate the rock into making the shot (or so I've always believed!).

HOG LINE

A line 33 feet from the hack that indicates the point by which a player must have released the handle of the rock. Rocks must also cross the hog line at the far end to remain in play, unless stopped on the line as the result of striking, or being struck by, another rock.

HOGGED

Of a rock, having failed to cross the far hog line. Hogged rocks are removed from play.

HOUSE

The series of four concentric circles at either end of the curling sheet.

IN-TURN

The spin applied to a curling rock by a curler when it is rotated towards the player's body. That is, right-handed players throw the rock with a clockwise motion, while left-handed players throw counter-clockwise.

LEAD

The player who throws the first two rocks of each end for his team.

MATE

Also called the third or the vice, the player who throws a team's fifth and sixth rocks in an end.

MEASURING STICK

The instrument used to determine which rock is closer to the centre of the house when it isn't possible to judge visually.

NEGATIVE ICE

A slant in the ice surface that may cause a rock to fall away, in the opposite direction to its curl.

OUT-TURN

The spin applied to a curling rock by a curler when it is rotated away from the player's body. That is, right-handed players throw the rock with a counter-clockwise motion, while left-handed players throw it clockwise.

PEBBLE

Small bumps on the ice surface, unique to curling ice and created when a fine spray of water is applied prior to a game. The pebble reduces friction, allowing the rock to glide much farther than it would over a smooth sheet of ice.

PEEL

An intentional shot that takes out both the opponent's rock and the delivered rock.

PICK

The unexpected change in rock direction, caused by debris on the ice.

PIN

The exact centre of the house.

PORT

An opening between two rocks that are in play.

RAISE

A stationary rock that is bumped forward by the delivered rock.

RAISED TAKEOUT

A rock that is knocked forward onto another rock with sufficient force to remove the latter from play.

ROCK

The common name for a curling stone.

SECOND

The player who delivers a team's third and fourth rocks of an end.

SHEET

The ice on which the game is played.

SIDELINE

The lines defining the boundaries of a sheet of ice.

SKIP

The player who generally delivers strategy for the team and indicates weight and line for the team's shots.

SLIDE PATH

The area close to the centre line, where the majority of play happens. The pebble wears down faster in the slide path; this affects the speed and curl of a rock as the game goes on.

SLIDER

The material on the sole of a curling shoe, usually Teflon, that allows curlers to slide along the ice.

SPLITTING THE HOUSE

The strategy of placing rocks on either side of the house.

SWEEPING

The process of cleaning, applying pressure, and applying friction to the ice in order to control the speed and degree of curl of a delivered rock.

TAKEOUT

A shot intended to strike a rock (generally an opponent's) in such a manner, and at such a speed, as to remove it from play.

TAP BACK

A shot that drives another rock towards the back of the house.

TEE LINE

The line that runs across the sheet, intersecting with the centre line at the pin.

THIRD

The player who throws a team's fifth and sixth rocks in an end. Also commonly called the vice or mate. The third acts as the skip when the skip is delivering his or her rocks and also assists in shot selection.

TICK

A shot that moves an opponent's first or second rock to a more favourable position on the sheet without removing it from the free guard zone. A term that has come into use since the introduction of the four-rock rule.

TWELVE-FOOT

The outermost circle in the house, 12 feet in diameter.

UP WEIGHT

Most teams tend to have a normal or control weight. If more weight is required, the curler will be asked to throw "up weight" or "peel weight."

WEIGHT

The amount of force with which a rock is delivered.

WICK

A thrown rock whose direction is altered slightly by grazing a stationary rock.

ZONE

In order to clearly communicate where a rock is required to stop, several teams have divided the area from the hog line through the house into numbered zones.

APPENDIX

CODE OF ETHICS

To ensure that all curlers are aware of their responsibilities when playing the game, the Canadian Curling Association has adopted the following Code of Ethics as an official supplement to the Rules of Curling for General Play:

Curlers' Code of Ethics

I will play the game with a spirit of good sportsmanship.

I will conduct myself in an honourable manner both on and off the ice.

I will never knowingly break a rule, but if I do, I will divulge the breach.

I will take no action that could be interpreted as an attempt to intimidate or demean my opponents, teammates or officials.

I will interpret the rules in an impartial manner, always keeping in mind that the purpose of the rules is to ensure that the game is played in an orderly and fair manner.

I will humbly accept any penalty that the governing body at any level of curling deems appropriate, if I am found in violation of the Code of Ethics or rules of the game.

Coaching Code of Ethics

The coach shall act with integrity in performing all duties owed to athletes, the sport, other members of the coaching profession and the public.

The coach shall strive to be well prepared and current in order that all duties in his/her discipline are fulfilled with competence.

The coach shall act in the best interest of the athlete's development as a whole person.

The coach shall accept both the letter and the spirit of the rules that define and govern the sport.

The coach shall accept the role of officials in providing judgment to ensure that competitions are conducted fairly and in accordance with the established rules.

The coach's conduct toward other coaches shall be characterized by courtesy, good faith and respect.

The coach shall maintain the highest standards of personal conduct and support the principles of Fair Play.

Fair Play

Fair Play begins with the strict observance of the written rule; however, in most cases, Fair Play involves something more than even unfailing observance of the written rule.

The observance of the spirit of the rules, whether written or unwritten, is important.

Fair Play results from measuring up to one's own moral standards while engaged in competition.

Fair Play is consistent demonstration of respect for teammates and opponents, whether they are winning or losing.

Fair Play is consistent demonstration of respect for officials, an acceptance of their decisions and a steadfast spirit of collaboration with them.

Sportsmanlike behaviour should be demonstrated both on and off the ice. This includes modesty in victory and composure in defeat.

RULES OF CURLING FOR GENERAL PLAY

1. Application

(1) The Rules of Curling for General Play apply to any competition to which they are made applicable by the curling body having jurisdiction.

(2) The Rules of Curling for General Play are not intended to be used in conjunction with officiating. If a curling body having jurisdiction over an event(s) wishes to make this rule book applicable to a specific competition(s) while also utilizing officials, they should also put in place a set of guidelines outlining the authority of the officials relative to the implementation of penalties.

(3) If special rules are in effect, they shall take precedence over the General Rules of Curling.

2. Definitions

(1) "biting" means that the vertical projection of a stone is in contact with the sheet line(s) to which the stone is in close proximity.

(2) "CCA" means the Canadian Curling Association.

(3) "competition" means a playdown involving any number of teams playing games to determine a winner.

(4) "counting stone" means any stationary stone in the house that is closer to the tee than any stationary stone of the opposing team.

(5) "delivering team" means the team who is in control of the house and whose turn it is to deliver.

(6) "end" means the part of the game in which two opposing teams each deliver eight stones alternately and then determine the score.

(7) "game" means play between two teams to determine a winner.

(8) "house" means the area within the outside circle at each end of the sheet.

(9) "sheet" means an area of ice marked in accordance with Rule 3.

(10) "delivered stone" means a stone that is in motion from the moment that it has reached the nearer tee line and been released, until it has come to rest or is out of play.

(11) "stone set in motion" means a stone in motion whose movement from a stationary position, in play, is caused by a delivered stone or another stone previously set in motion.

(12) "team" means three or four players playing together in accordance with Rule 5 and may also include the team alternate and coach as determined by the rules of the competition.

(13) "original position" means the position the stones were in immediately before the violation or incident took place.

3. Sheet

(1) The recommended length of the sheet from backboard to backboard shall be 146 feet (44.501 metres). The width of the sheet from sideline to sideline shall be a minimum of

14 feet 2 inches (4.318 metres) and a maximum of 16 feet 5 inches (5.0038 metres) for championship play. This area shall be delineated by lines drawn or dividers placed on the perimeter.

(2) The centre line, one-half inch in width, shall be placed the length of the sheet through the centre of the tee lines to a point 12 feet (3.658 metres) behind each tee. At this point, a line one-half inch in width (1.27 centimetres) and 1 foot 6 inches (45.72 centimetres) in length shall be placed at right angles to the centre line and shall be known as the hack line. The inside (circle side) edge of the hack boards shall be placed on this hack line.

(3) At each end of the sheet there shall be three distinct lines drawn from sideline to sideline as follows:

(a) each tee line, one-half inch in width, shall be placed 12 feet (3.658 metres) from the hack line to the centre of the tee line and there shall be 114 feet (34.747 metres) from the centre of one tee line to the centre of the other tee line. The distance from the backboard to the centre of the tee line shall be 16 feet (4.877 metres) if the length of the sheet is 146 feet (44.501 metres) from backboard to backboard. The intersection of the tee line and the centre line is called the tee.

(b) each back line, one-half inch in width, shall be placed with its outer edge 6 feet (1.829 metres) from the centre of the tee line, so that the outer edge of the back line (hack side) is a tangent with the 12 foot circle touching the outer edge of the outer circle exactly 6 feet (1.829 metres) from the tee, where the back line intersects the centre line.

(c) the hog line, 4 inches (10.16 centimetres) in width, shall be placed with the inner (circle side) edge 21 feet (6.401 metres) from the centre of the tee line.

(4) With each tee as centre, there shall be drawn four concentric circles at each end with the outer edge of the outer circle having a radius of 6 feet (1.829 metres), the next circle 4 feet (1.219 metres), the next circle 2 feet (60.96 centimetres) and the inner circle a minimum of 6 inches (15.24 centimetres). The marking of the centre line and tee line may be omitted from the inner circle.

(5) The intersection of each tee line and each centre line shall be identified by an adjustable tee centre. The base portion shall be securely anchored at the exact intersection of the tee line and centre line of each house, and the top portion should be capable of vertical

adjustment to suit varying ice levels. The design of the tee centre shall be accepted by the CCA.

(6) The hack(s) used for delivery shall be of a style and size accepted by the CCA. The hack(s) shall not exceed 8 inches (20.32 centimetres) in length.

(a) If two hacks are used, the back edge of each hack shall be placed on the hack lines and that the inside edge of each hack shall be no further than 3 inches (7.62 centimetres) from the centre line.

(b) If one moveable hack is used, it shall be placed with the back edge of the hack on the hack line and be either centered on the centre line or with the inside edge no further than 3 inches (7.62 centimetres) from the centre line (left or right).

(c) If one fixed hack is used, it shall be placed with the back edge of the hack on the hack line and centered on the centre line.

4. Stones

(1) Curling stones shall be of circular shape.

(2) Curling stones, including handle and bolt, shall weigh a maximum of 44 lbs. (19.96 kilograms) and a minimum of 38.5 lbs. (17.46 kilograms), shall have a maximum circumference of 36 inches (91.44 centimetres) and shall be a maximum of 5.5 inches (13.97 centimetres) in height, measured between the bottom and top of the stone.

(3) Two sets of eight stones shall be provided for each sheet of play.

(4) A team member or coach shall not physically alter the running surface or weight of either teams' assigned or selected game stones in any manner.

(5) If a stone is broken in play, a replacement stone shall be placed where the largest fragment comes to rest. The inside edge of the replacement stone shall be placed in the same position as the inside edge of the largest fragment with the assistance of a measuring stick.

(6) A stone that rolls over in its course or comes to rest on its side or top shall be removed immediately from play.

(7) All 16 stones originally on the sheet at the start of a game shall be delivered in every completed end. No interchange of stones or redelivery of previously delivered stones in

that end may take place so that a stone is delivered for the second time.

Penalty: If a team declares its own violation of Rule 4(7), the non-offending team may allow the play to stand or remove the stone just delivered from play and replace all affected stones as close as possible to their original positions.

5. Teams

(1) Every team shall be composed of a minimum of four players as determined by the rules of the competition except as provided for in Rule 5(5). Prior to each game, the team shall designate the four eligible members of the team who will commence play as players for that team.

(2) Unless otherwise specified in the rules of the competition:

(a) the teams opposing each other in a game shall toss a coin to determine which team plays the first stone in the first end. The winner of the toss has the choice between playing the first or second stone of the end; and

(b) the team that plays the first stone of the end has choice of handle colour.

In the second and subsequent ends, the winner of the preceding end shall play the first stone of the end.

(3) Each player on a four player team shall deliver two stones in each end alternately with his/her opponent.

(4) The delivery rotation declared by a team prior to the start of a game shall be followed throughout that game except as provided for in Rule 5(5), 5(6) or 5(7).

(5) Unless otherwise specified in the rules of the competition:

(a) A team shall include a minimum of two players from the original team and a substitute player(s). A team that is missing a player(s) may use a substitute player(s).

(b) A substitute player shall be a team's designated alternate, a player from a players pool or other eligible player as provided for in the rules of the competition.

(c) A team may play with three players with the first two players each delivering three stones in each end. Under no circumstance may a team play with fewer than three players delivering stones.

(d) A substitute player who joins a team prior to the start of a game may deliver stones in any position of the delivery rotation of the team. The team shall declare their delivery rotation at this time.

(e) A substitute player who joins a team between ends may deliver stones in any position of the delivery rotation of his/her team. Players may move up or down the delivery rotation only as required to position the substitute player and the team shall re-declare their delivery rotation at this time.

(f) During an end in play, if a player(s) is unable to complete the delivery rotation declared by the team at the start of the game the team may activate a substitute player(s) subject to:

> i) a substitute player may only enter a game during an end if they deliver a stone within that end; and

> ii) a substitute player(s) who enters a game during an end shall replace the sidelined player(s) in the team's delivery rotation for that end; and

> iii) at the beginning of the next end the substitute player may deliver stones in any position of the delivery rotation of his/her team. Players may move up or down in the delivery rotation only as required to position the substitute player and the team shall re-declare their delivery rotation at this time; and

> iv) the replaced team member shall not rejoin the team until the next game unless the team loses a subsequent player(s) and is therefore placed in a default position as per Rule 5(5)(a) and (b).

(6) (a) A team that commences a game with three players and expects the fourth player to join the team during the game shall establish the team's four player delivery rotation prior to commencing the game.

(b) A player who is late for a game may enter the game between ends or may enter an end already in progress providing he/she is able to deliver a stone within the team's established delivery rotation.

(c) A player who has left a game may re-enter the game between ends or during an end already in progress providing he/she is able to deliver a stone within the team's established delivery rotation. If a substitute player has been activated, the replaced team member shall not rejoin the team until the next game except as provided in Rule 5(5)(f) iv).

(7) (a) If a player delivers his/her first stone of the end and is unable to deliver his/her

second stone of the end and the rules of the competition allow the team to continue play with three players and the team chooses to play with three players, the following procedures shall be followed:

- If the lead player, the second player shall deliver the lead player's stone.
- If the second player, the lead player shall deliver the second player's stone.
- If the third player, the second player shall deliver the third player's stone.
- If the fourth player, the third player shall deliver the fourth player's stone.

(b) If a player is unable to deliver both his/her stones during an end and the rules of the competition allow the team to continue with three players and the team chooses to play with three players, the following procedures shall be followed for the end in progress:

- If the lead player, the second player shall deliver both of the lead player's stones and one of the second player's stones, and the third player shall deliver one of the second player's stones and both of the third player's stones.
- If the second player, the lead player shall deliver the first of the second player's stones, and the third player shall deliver the second of the second player's stones and both of the third player's stones.
- If the third player, the second player shall deliver both of the third player's stones.
- If the fourth player, the third player shall deliver both of the fourth player's stones.

Penalty: If a team declares its own violation of Rule 5(4), 5(5), 5(6), or 5(7), all stones shall be allowed to come to rest before any action is taken. At this time, the non-offending team may allow the play to stand or remove the stone just delivered from play and replace all affected stones as close as possible to their original positions.

6. Skips

(1) The skip has the exclusive direction of the game for his/her team and shall deliver stones in each end except as provided for in Rule 5(7).

(2) Subject to Rule 5(4), the skip may play any position in the delivery rotation of his/her team. Regardless of the position played in the delivery rotation, the player designated as skip shall remain in that capacity throughout the course of that game except as provided for in Rule 5(6).

(3) When it is the skip's turn to deliver, he/she shall elect a teammate to act as skip. Subject to Rule 5(4), the vice-skip may play any position in the delivery rotation of his/her team. Regardless of the position played in the delivery rotation, the player designated as vice-skip shall remain in that capacity throughout the course of that game except as provided for in Rule 5(6). The vice-skip shall assume the responsibilities of the skip when the skip is not on the playing surface.

Penalty: If a team declares its own violation of Rule 6(1), 6(2) or 6(3), all stones shall be allowed to come to rest before any action is taken. At this time, the nonoffending team may allow the play to stand or remove the stone just delivered from play and replace all affected stones as close as possible to their original positions.

7. Position of Players

(1) Members of the non-delivering team:

(a) The skip and vice-skip and only the skip and vice-skip may be positioned inside the hog line at the playing end and shall position themselves behind the back line when the delivering team is in the process of delivery. Both players shall be motionless with their brooms positioned in a manner not to interfere with or distract the attention of the player who is in the process of delivery as provided for in Rule 8(2).

(b) One player may take a stationary position by the backboard at the delivering end and to the side of the sheet. The player shall remain silent and motionless when the delivering team player is in the process of delivery as provided for in Rule 8(2).

(c) The players not taking the positions 7(1)(a) or 7(1)(b) shall position themselves between the hog lines and to the extreme sides of the sheet when the opposing team is delivering a stone. The players positioned in this area shall remain in single file when the delivering team player is in the process of delivery as provided for in Rule 8(2).

(d) The non-delivering team members shall not take any position or cause such motion that would obstruct, interfere with or distract any member of the delivering team.

Penalty: If a team declares its own violation of Rule 7(1)(a), 7(1)(b), 7(1)(c) or 7(1)(d), all stones shall be allowed to come to rest before any action is taken. At this time, the non-offending team has the option of:

i) allowing the play to stand; or

ii) recommencing the delivery of the stone; or

iii) replacing all affected stones as close as possible to their original position and redelivering the stone

(2) Members of the delivering team:

(a) The skip or vice-skip shall be positioned inside the hog line and on the ice surface of the playing end while their team is in the process of delivery. They shall have choice of position for the purpose of directing play.

Penalty: If a team declares its own violation of Rule 7(2)(a), all stones shall be allowed to come to rest before any action is taken. At this time, the nonoffending team may allow the play to stand or remove the stone just delivered from play and replace all affected stones as close as possible to their original positions.

8. Delivery

(1) Only right-handed deliveries shall be initiated from the hack located to the left of the centre line and only left-handed deliveries shall be initiated from the hack located to the right of the centre line. Both right-handed and left-handed deliveries may be initiated from a hack located on the centre line.

Interpretation: If a single, moveable hack is in use it shall be positioned as required by the delivering team in accordance with Rule 3(6) and 8(1).

Interpretation: The delivery and release of a curling stone are intended to occur within a reasonable proximity to the centre line.

Penalty: If a team declares its own violation of Rule 8(1), all stones shall be allowed to come to rest before any action is taken. At this time, the nonoffending team may allow the play to stand or remove the stone just delivered from play and replace all affected stones as close as possible to their original positions.

(2) (a) A player whose team is in control of the house is deemed to be in the process of delivery from the time the player is positioned in the hack until the stone is released.

(b) A player shall only commence a forward progression from the hack with a stone after the previously delivered stone and any stones set in motion have come to rest or have crossed the back line and his/her team is in control of the house.

(3) In the delivery, the stone shall be released before it has reached the nearer hog line.

Penalty: The delivered stone and all affected stones shall be allowed to come to rest before any action is taken. If a team declares its own violation of Rule 8(3), the non-offending team shall remove the stone just delivered from play and replace all affected stones as close as possible to their original positions.

(4) If a player wishes to recommence the delivery as a result of his/her own team's action, the player may do so providing the stone has not reached the nearer tee line.
Interpretation: The delivery may be recommenced if the player's body or equipment reaches the tee line providing the stone does not.

(5) If an extreme circumstance occurs during the delivery that distracts the thrower to a significant degree during the process of delivery [Rule 8(2)], the stone may be redelivered prior to the opposition delivering their next stone.

(6) Each player shall be ready to deliver when his/her turn comes.

(7) Delay of a game in progress by a player for any reason excluding accident or illness shall not exceed three minutes.

(8) If a player delivers a stone belonging to the opposing team, a stone belonging to his/her team shall be put in its place.

(9) (a) If a player delivers a stone out of proper rotation, the end shall continue and the delivery rotation shall continue to be in accordance with Rule 5(3) and 5(4), except as provided for in rule 5(7).
Interpretation: This includes the situation when the team with last stone throws first.
(b) If an error in delivery rotation causes a player on the same team to miss a turn, the player who has missed a turn shall deliver the last stone for his/her team in the end.
Interpretation: This rule applies to the situation when the second player delivers the lead player's second stone and other similar delivery rotation errors.

(10) If the opposing teams agree that a stone has been missed but are unable to determine which player missed his/her turn, the lead of the team that missed a turn shall play the last stone for his/her team in that end.

(11) (a) If a team delivers two stones in succession in the same end, they shall remove the second stone that was played, replace any stone(s) displaced by the stone and the end shall continue. The delivery rotation of the offending team shall be altered for that end so that the player who delivered the second of the two stones delivered in succession

shall deliver the last stone for his/her team in that end.

(b) If the non-offending team delivers a stone prior to the error in delivery rotation being detected, the end shall be continued. If the non-offending team has last stone they shall deliver the last two stones of the end in succession. If the non-offending team is the team who started the end without last stone they shall deliver the last stone of the end.

(12) If a player on a four player team delivers three stones in one end, except as provided for in Rule 5(7), the end shall be continued and the fourth player on the offending team shall deliver one stone only in that end.

(13) If the handle came off of a stone during the process of the delivery [Rule 8(2)], the delivering team may:

(i) allow the play to stand, or

(ii) redeliver the stone after all affected stones have been replaced as close as possible to their original position.

The delivering team must make their choice prior to the opposition delivering their next stone. *Interpretation*: This does not apply to a handle that is loose but did not separate from the stone.

9. Touched Delivered Stone or Stone(s) Set in Motion

(1) A delivered stone or stone set in motion shall not be touched by any player, equipment or personal belongings of the team to which it belongs.

Interpretation: A stone which has been released (fingers and thumb no longer in contact with the handle) and then retouched by the delivering player is considered a touched delivered stone and thus a breach of Rule 9(1). A player who repositions his/her hand on the handle while in the process of delivery and does so without losing contact with the handle is not in breach of Rule 9(1).

Penalty: If the violation occurs after the stone has been released, all stones shall be allowed to come to rest before any action is taken. If a team declares its own violation of Rule 9(1) the non-offending team may then remove the touched stone from play and replace all affected stones as close as possible to their original positions unless they select either of these alternative options:

i) allowing the play to stand; or

ii) placing the touched stone and all stones it would have affected where they would have come to rest had the violation not occurred. This option is only applicable where the violation occurred inside the hog line at the end of play or involved a stone considered to be in play.

(2) A delivered stone shall not be touched by any player of the opposing team or their equipment nor shall they cause the stone to be touched.

Penalty: All stones shall be allowed to come to rest before any action is taken. If a team declares its own violation of Rule 9(2) the non-offending team has the option of:

i) allowing the play to stand; or

ii) replacing all affected stones as close as possible to their original position and redelivering the stone; or

iii) placing the touched stone and all stones it affected or would have affected where they would have come to rest had the violation not occurred. This option is only applicable where the violation occurred inside the hog line at the end of play or involved a stone considered to be in play.

(3) A stone set in motion shall not be touched by any player of the opposing team or their equipment nor shall they cause the stone to be touched.

Penalty: All stones shall be allowed to come to rest before any action is taken. If a team declares its own violation of Rule 9(3), the non-offending team has the option of:

i) allowing the play to stand; or

ii) placing the touched stone and all stones it affected or would have affected where they would have come to rest had the violation not occurred.

(4) If a delivered stone or stone in the process of delivery was touched or caused to be touched by an external force, i.e. stone, broom or brush from another sheet, spectator, etc., the player shall redeliver the stone. If the touched stone has displaced other stones, they shall be replaced as close as possible to their original positions to the satisfaction of both teams.

(5) If a stone(s) set in motion was touched or caused to be touched by an external force, the stone(s) set in motion and all stones they would have affected shall be placed where they would have come to rest had the incident not occurred with placement to the satisfaction of both teams.

10. Displaced Stationary Stones

(1) A stationary stone shall not be displaced by a player or that player's equipment nor shall a player cause a stone to be displaced by an opposing player or that player's equipment.

Penalty—Situation #1: If a team declares its own violation of Rule 10(1), and the displaced stone did not alter and would not have altered the course of a delivered stone or stone in motion,

i)the non-offending team shall replace the displaced stone(s) as close as possible to its original position, and

ii) if the displacement occurred while playing the final stone of the end and/or prior to agreement of the score, Rule 13(9) shall apply.

Interpretation: If there is any question as to which stone(s) was closer to the tee, the displaced stone shall be positioned in favour of the non-offending team.

Penalty—Situation #2: If a team declares its own violation of Rule 10(1) and the displaced stationary stone altered or would have altered the course of a delivered stone or stone set in motion, all stones shall be allowed to come to rest before any action is taken. At this time the non-offending team has the option of

i) allowing the play to stand; or

ii) placing the stone just delivered or stone set in motion and all stones it would have affected where they would have come to rest had the violation not occurred; or

iii) removing the stone just delivered or stone set in motion from play and replacing all affected stones as close as possible to their original positions. Interpretation: If there is any question as to which stone(s) would have been closer to the tee had the violation not occurred, the stone(s) that was affected or would have been affected by the delivered stone or stone set in motion shall be positioned in favor of the non-offending team.

(2) The delivering team shall prevent a stationary stone(s) from being displaced by a stone(s) that is deflected from a divider or from a stationary stone on another sheet.

Penalty: If a team declares its own violation of Rule 10(2), all stones shall be allowed to come to rest before any action is taken. At this time the nonoffending team shall replace the displaced stationary stone(s) as close as possible to its original position. If the displacement occurred while playing the final stone of an end and prior to agreement of the score, Rule 13(9) shall apply.

Interpretation: If there is any question as to which stone(s) was closer to the tee or would have been closer to the tee had the violation not occurred, the displaced stone(s) or stone(s) in motion shall be positioned in favor of the non-offending team.

(3) If the stones are displaced during an end in a way other than stated in the preceding rules, the teams shall determine the positions to which the stones are to be returned, subject to:

a) If the teams cannot agree on the original position of the displaced stones relative to which was closer to the tee, the end shall be replayed; and

b) If the displacement occurred at the conclusion of play in an end and prior to agreement of the score, Rule 13(9) shall apply.

11. Sweeping/Brushing

(1) Between the tee lines, all members of the delivering team may sweep/brush any of their team's stones that have been delivered or set in motion.

Interpretation: A stationary stone must be set in motion before any sweeping may occur.

(2) Only the skip or vice-skip of the non-delivering team may sweep/brush their team's stone(s) after it is set in motion.

(3) Behind the tee line, only one player from each team may brush at one time. This may be the skip or vice-skip of either team or the lead or second of the delivering team.

Interpretation: The only time a lead or second of the delivering team may sweep/brush behind the tee line is when sweeping/brushing his/her team's delivered stone or any stone set in motion.

(4) Behind the tee line, the delivering team shall have first privilege of sweeping/brushing any stone. If their choice is not to sweep/brush, they shall not obstruct or prevent the non-delivering skip or vice skip from sweeping/brushing the stone.

(5) An opponent's delivered stone or stone set in motion shall not be swept/brushed until it reaches the farther tee line and sweeping/brushing shall only take place behind the tee line.

Penalty: If a team declares its own violation of Rule 11(1), 11(2), 11(3), 11(4) or 11(5), all stones shall be allowed to come to rest before any action is taken. At this time the non-offending team may allow the play to stand or place the stone and all stones it would have affected where they would have come to rest had the sweeping violation not occurred.

(6)(a) The sweeping/brushing motion shall be in a side to side direction but is not required to cover the entire width of the stone.

(b) The sweeping/brushing motion shall not leave any debris in front of a delivered stone or stone set in motion.

(c) The final sweeping/brushing motion shall finish to either side of the delivered stone or stone set in motion.

(7) All sweeping/brushing shall take place in front of the delivered stone or stone set in motion and within 6 feet (1.83 metres) of the stone.

(8) When sweeping with a corn/straw broom, the sweeping motion shall take place with the corn/straw pointing in the direction of play.

Interpretation: Backward sweeping with a corn/straw broom is not acceptable.

Penalty: If a team declares its own violation of Rule 11(6), 11(7) or 11(8), all stones shall be allowed to come to rest before any action is taken. At this time the non-offending team has the option of

i) allowing the play to stand; or

ii) removing the unfairly swept/brushed stone from play and replacing all affected stones as close as possible to their original position; or iii) placing the unfairly swept/brushed stone and stone(s) it would have affected where they would have come to rest had the sweeping/brushing violation not occurred.

12. Free Guard Zone

(1) The free guard zone is the area between the hog line and the tee line, excluding the house.

Interpretation: A stone which comes to rest biting or in front of the hog line after making contact with a stone in the free guard zone is considered to be in the free guard zone. A stone which comes to rest outside the house but biting the tee line is not considered to be in the free guard zone.

(2) Any stationary stone(s) belonging to the opposition that is located in the free guard zone shall not be moved to an out-of-play position by the delivering team prior to the delivery of the 5th stone of the end.

Penalty: A stone that is delivered prior to the 5th stone of the end that results in an opposition stone being moved from the free guard zone, either directly or indirectly, to an out-of-play position is an infraction which shall result in the delivered stone being removed from play and any other stone if moved being replaced as close as possible to its original position.

Interpretation: A delivered third or fourth stone of an end may hit an opposition stone(s) located in the free guard zone on to a stone(s) not in the free guard zone providing that any opposition stone originally located in the free guard zone remains in play. If this action results in an opposition free guard zone stone being moved to an out-of-play position, the penalty described above will apply. You may move your own stone from the free guard zone or remove your own stone from the free guard zone, providing you do not cause an opposition stone to be moved from the free guard zone to an out-of-play position. You may also raise your stone located in the free guard zone onto an opposition stone located in the house and remove it from play.

(3) After the delivery of each of the first three stones of an end it is the responsibility of the skip of the team who is about to deliver to ensure agreement with the opposing skip as to whether or not any of the stone(s) in play have come to rest in the free guard zone. If they cannot agree, they may make the determination by using the six foot measuring stick. If the position of another stone(s) hinders the use of the six foot measure they may reposition the stone(s), complete the measurement and replace the stone(s) to its original position.

(4) A visual agreement by the opposing skips as to whether or not one of the first three stones of the end was in the free guard zone, does not preclude a measurement occurring at the conclusion of the end involving the same stone(s).

13. Stones in Play and Scoring

(1) A stone that does not come to rest inside the inner edge (house side) of the farther hog line shall be removed from play immediately except where it has struck another stone lying in play.

Interpretation: A stone which crosses the hog line but, when stopping, spins such that it comes to rest biting the hog line, is considered "out of play."

(2) A stone coming to rest beyond the outer edge of the back line shall be immediately removed from play.
Interpretation: A stone which crosses the back line but, when stopping, spins such that it comes to rest biting the back line, is considered "in play."

(3) A stone that touches a sideline, hits a divider or comes to rest biting a sideline shall be removed immediately from play.
Interpretation: If a delivered stone or stone in motion hits a stationary stone and a sideline or divider at the same time, the stationary stone shall be allowed to take its course as if it had been hit first.

(4) A game shall be decided by a majority of points.

(5) Each stone, any part of which is within 6 feet (1.83 metres) of the tee, is eligible to be counted.

(6) A team scores one point for each eligible stone that is closer to the tee than any stone of the opposing team.

(7) An end shall be decided when the skips or vice-skips in charge of the house at the time agree upon the score for the end.

(8) If two or more stones are tied, then none of the tied stones shall count and only stones closer to the tee than the tied stones shall be eligible to be counted. If the tied stones are to determine which team shall count in that end, the end shall be considered blank.

(9) If a stone(s) which may have affected the points scored in an end is displaced prior to the skips or vice-skips deciding the score, the team causing the displacement shall forfeit the point(s) involved.

(10) Should an individual other than the two teams or their coaches displace or cause the displacement of a stone(s) prior to agreement of the score or a measure being determined, the following shall apply:

(a) Preceding the final end;

(i) If the displaced stone(s) would have determined who won an end, the end shall be replayed.

(ii) If a team secured a point(s) and the displaced stone(s) would have determined if an additional point(s) was scored, that team shall have the option of replaying the end or keeping the point(s) already secured and proceeding to the next end.

(b) In the final end:

(i) If the game is tied and the displaced stone(s) would have determined which team won the game, the end shall be replayed.

(ii) If the displaced stone(s) would have determined if the game was tied or lost by the team that was behind in points, that team shall have the option of replaying the end or keeping the point(s) they had secured and playing another end without last rock.

(iii) If the team that was behind in points had already secured sufficient points to tie the game, and the displaced stone(s) would have determined if they won the game, that team shall have the option of replaying the end or keeping the point(s) already secured and playing an additional end, with last rock being determined by a single draw to the tee with sweeping/brushing. The team who was ahead in points when the end began shall have the choice of drawing first or last.

(iv) If the displaced stone(s) would have determined if the game was lost, tied or won, the team that was down in points shall have the option of replaying the end or keeping the point(s) already secured, if any, and playing an additional end, with last rock being determined by a single draw to the tee with sweeping/brushing. The team who was ahead in points when the end began shall have the choice of drawing first or last.

Interpretation: Rule 13(10)(b)(iv) applies to the following types of situations:

• A team is one down going home and measuring two of their stones to determine if they have lost, tied or won the game.

• A team is two down going home counting one and measuring two of their stones to determine if they have lost, tied or won the game.

(11) If after regulation play [Rule 16(1)], the score is tied, play shall be continued without changing the rotation of play (end the stones are thrown to) for such additional end or ends as may be required to decide the winning team.

14. Measuring

(1) Measurements shall be taken from the tee to the closest part of the stone.

Interpretation: Because stones may vary in diameter, measurements shall not be taken from the tee to the farthest part of a stone.

(2) No physical device to aid visual observation shall be used in measuring prior to the last

stone delivered in the end coming to rest except as provided for in Rule 12(3) and 14(4).

(3) Decisions on whether a stone is in or out of play at the hog line, sidelines and back line shall be visual (no accepted measuring device) except as provided for in Rule 14(4). If the opposing skips cannot agree, they may request a nonpartisan third party to render a decision.

(4) A skip may conduct a measurement when a stone is located on the back line in proximity to the centre line (6:00 position) to confirm if the stone is in or out of play. The 6 foot (1.83 metres) measuring stick shall be used.

Interpretation: If the position of a stone(s) in the house makes it impossible to use the measuring stick to determine if a stone is in or out of play and the opposing skips cannot agree, they may request a non-partisan third party to render a decision.

(5) If two or more stones are so close to the tee that a measuring device cannot be used, and if a visual comparison cannot determine which stone is closest to the tee, the stones shall be considered tied. If these stones were to determine who counted in the end, the end shall be considered blank.

(6) A measuring stick that measures a distance of six feet (1.83 metres) from the tee shall be used, if necessary, to confirm whether a stone is within six feet (1.83 metres) of the tee as provided for in Rule 12(2), 13(5) and 14(4).

15. Equipment

(1) A player shall not use footwear or equipment that may damage or affect the playing quality of the ice surface. (Examples: excessive debris from a corn/straw broom, shedding brushes, faulty slider or gripper.)

(2) At the start of each game, each player shall declare what type of sweeping/brushing device that he/she shall be using for the duration of the game (brush, synthetic straw style broom or corn/straw broom). Players may change or exchange brushes, brush heads and synthetic straw style brooms during a game. Players shall use the same corn/straw broom for the duration of the game and shall not exchange a corn/straw broom with another player.

(3) A broom or brush broken during the game shall be replaced by the same type of sweeping/brushing device.

(4) The use of a curling aid commonly referred to as a "delivery stick" which enables

the player to deliver a stone without placing a hand on the handle is considered acceptable. If a player starts a game with a delivery stick then that player shall use a delivery stick throughout that game. If a player starts a game without a delivery stick, then a delivery stick shall not be used by that player in that game.
Interpretation: All traditional delivery rules apply and the stone must be delivered along a straight line from the hack to the intended target brush/broom.

(5) The use of a curling aid commonly referred to as a "delivery balance device" is considered acceptable. The balance device shall not exceed 5 feet (152.4 centimetres) in length and 12 inches (30.5 centimetres) in width. Height may vary.

16. Game Duration and Postponement

(1) A game shall be of such length or duration as is stated in the rules governing the competition.

(2) If for any reason a game is postponed to another time, the game shall continue from the last completed end.

(3) If a team does not commence play at the designated time, unless otherwise stated by the rules governing the competition:
i) For each full five minutes that the offending team does not commence play, the non-offending team shall be granted one point and one end shall be considered to have been played; and
ii) If the non-offending team has been granted a point(s), they shall be given the choice of last rock in the first end or color of handle. Play shall commence from the end of play that reflects the number of ends that are considered to have been played; and
iii) After 30 minutes has elapsed the non-offending team shall be declared the winner.

17. Wheelchair Curling

(1) Stones are delivered from a stationary wheelchair and the stone must be positioned within 18 inches (45.72 cm) of the centre line. Curling clubs that have active wheelchair programs or clubs hosting wheelchair competitions should install two (2) lines eighteen (18) inches (45.72 cm) on either side of the centre line running from the inside edge of the hog line to the outside edge of the twelve (12) foot circle.

(2) During delivery, the wheels of the chair must be in direct contact with the ice and the feet of the player delivering the stone must not touch the ice surface during delivery.

(3) The delivery of the stone is undertaken by the conventional arm/hand release, or by the use of an approved delivery stick.

(4) Stones must be clearly released from the hand or stick before the stone reaches the hog line at the delivering end.

(5) A stone is in play when it reaches the hog line at the delivering end. A stone that has not reached the hog line at the delivering end may be returned to the player and redelivered.

(6) Sweeping is not permitted.

18. Miscellaneous

(1) If any exceptions to the preceding rules are necessary to accommodate players with physical disabilities, appropriate adjustments are considered acceptable.

(2) Should any situation occur that is not covered by the rules, the decision shall be made in accordance with equity.

Canadian Curling Association's (CCA) Rules of Curling for General Play and Code of Ethics reprinted courtesy of the CCA

ACKNOWLEDGEMENTS

I've had the privilege of playing the game I love for more than 40 years. The grand old game of curling has brought me so many memories, friendships and experiences, so it was thrilling to be asked to share what I know about the game I love.

This is my second book, and I wish to thank the team behind it. Thank you to Abbie Darnley and the High Park Curling Club for assisting in the photo shoot (and for demonstrating terrific brushing technique too!), Michael Burns, Adrienne Leahy, Paul Arsenault, Dale Matchett, and Elliott Kerr. And thanks to the team at HarperCollins, including Brad Wilson, Iris Tupholme, Noelle Zitzer, Neil Erickson, Greg Tabor, Lloyd Davis, and Barbara Kamienski.

To my teammates, past and present, it's been inspiring and a honour to play with you. I'm grateful that some of my fellow curlers have kindly contributed to this book. Thank you to Wade Blanchard, Mark Dacey, Brad Gushue, Toby McDonald, and Kelly Scott.

Above all, my continued love and gratitude to the entire Team Howard.

Hurry hard!

INDEX